Mosaic

Mosaic

A Million Little Pieces

ARVILLA FEE

Foreword by Mac Sandlin

RESOURCE *Publications* · Eugene, Oregon

MOSAIC
A Million Little Pieces

Copyright © 2024 Arvilla Fee. All rights reserved. Except for brief quotations in critical publications or reviews, no part of this book may be reproduced in any manner without prior written permission from the publisher. Write: Permissions, Wipf and Stock Publishers, 199 W. 8th Ave., Suite 3, Eugene, OR 97401.

Resource Publications
An Imprint of Wipf and Stock Publishers
199 W. 8th Ave., Suite 3
Eugene, OR 97401

www.wipfandstock.com

PAPERBACK ISBN: 979-8-3852-3924-5
HARDCOVER ISBN: 979-8-3852-3925-2
EBOOK ISBN: 979-8-3852-3926-9

12/06/24

Contents

Acknowledgments	xi
Foreword by Mac Sandlin	xiii
Preface	xv
Pieces	xvii

PART I | A MILLION SORROWS

An Adage of Untruth	3
All Is Fair	4
Butterfly	5
The Cabin Cat	6
Delivery People	7
Embedded	8
Fade to Black	9
The Fall of Us	10
The Greatest Grief	11
I Grew Thin	12
Innocence Lost	13
In the Dark	14
The Love and Loss of a Dog	15
Meet Me by the River	16
My Skin Feels Slick with Grief	18
No Words	19
Oh, Child of Mine	20

Contents

Patterns	21
Phantom Pain	22
Ribs	23
Shadow Girl	24
Some Things Won't Bear the Weight of Words	25
The Sun Always Rises	26
The Thin Quest	28
A Trap of Your Own Making	29
The Urns We Carry	30
The Way Back	31
You Know	33

PART II | A MILLION YESTERDAYS

After Apocalypse	37
The American Barn	38
The Apple Peeler	39
As the Candle Burns	40
Baker's Cabinet	41
Beginnings Triolet	42
A Betrayal of Bones	43
The Breath	44
Clementine Stockings	45
Crawdads and Bologna	46
A Division of Goods	48
Dust to Dust	50
Forever Eighteen	51
The Gap	52
Genetics	53
The Golden Young	54
The Grudge	55
The Hands that Held	56
If You Decide to Go	57

I Wish You Could've Stayed	58
Kansas 1935	59
The Keeping Room	60
The Last Drive-In Movie Theater	61
Leftovers	62
Lost Libraries	63
Our Cup of Coffee	64
Passed Down	65
Remembering I Don't Remember	66
Reversal of Roles	67
There's a Meadow	68
Too Young to Know	70
Unmended	71
We Used To	72
When My Metabolism was Young	73
Worn around the Edges	74
You Once Told Me I Was Beautiful	75

PART III | A MILLION LIVES

The 1930s Auntie Brigade	79
Aging out	81
The Ballad of Returning Soldiers	82
Bartender	84
The Blind Man's Nose	85
Cold Shoulder	86
Dear Daughter	87
Dear John Donne	88
Donation Tuesdays	89
Everyone Smiles But the Clown	90
Final Symphony	91
The Honeybee Box	92
The Kindness Experiment	93

Contents

Light from Within	95
Mama and Papa's Dance	97
My Father, the Lonely Mechanic	99
Neurodivergent Processing	100
Once Around the Block	102
Polishing Stars	103
Recall of a Soldier	104
Runner	105
Secret Faith	106
Send It	107
Spanish Moss Chronicles	108
Sketching	109
Subway Blessing	110
The Talisman	112
Though We Don't Speak the Same Language	113
Unconventional Education	114
Upon This I Hitched My Dreams	115
Waiting for the Diagnosis	116
The Way of Water Pots	118
When You Call Me Momma	119
Where Dreams Are Made	120

PART IV | A MILLION NATURES

Beneath the Surface	125
Bonfire Triolet	126
Chamomile and Poetry	127
Confessional	128
Hope Comes in Yellow	129
The Lovely Alone	130
My Trip to the Moon Triolet	131
Recovery	132
Room to Breathe	133

A Serengeti Corn Field	134
Shedding	135
Stepping Back	136
Tender Year	137
Time Out	138
These Brave Branches	139
Wasting Days Triolet	140
Winter Solstice	141
Winter Weight	143

PART V | A MILLION GIGGLES

35th Class Reunion	147
All in the Family	149
The Best Exes	150
A Boy's Pockets	151
Buffering	152
Can I Get a Refund?	153
A Card-Carrying Member of the Passive Aggressive Club	154
Comfort Food	155
Counting Geese	156
Does Wanting Count?	157
Enlighten Me	158
The Face of a Thousand Words	159
Get a Cat They Said	160
I'm Old Enough	161
The Introverted Extrovert	162
I Used to	163
Just South of Sanity	164
The Longest Ride	165
The Luckiest Girl Triolet	167
Midnight Maze	168
My Conversation with an Earthworm	169

CONTENTS

Oh, Emily	170
Perhaps God Is Waiting for a Hallelujah	171
Please Excuse My OCD	172
The Recipe of My Tribe	173
Running Late	174
A Single Crow	175
Too Peopley Out There	176

PART VI | A MILLION TRIUMPHS

Beautiful Barbed Wire	179
Building Bridges	180
Cry Me a River	181
Did I	182
Expectations	183
Ghosted	184
The Great Awakening	185
The Houses I Built	186
The Hummingbirds Will Return	187
I'm Alone but Not Lonely	188
Invincible Summer	189
Line in the Sand	190
Not the End of My Story	191
There's Something about the Rearview	192
The Underdog	193
What a Beautiful Mess	195
Woman from the Rib	196
A Work in Progress	198
You Will Look	199
Acknowledgments	201
About the Author	209

Acknowledgments

I'm thankful for God and His amazing grace. For my mom, Shirley; my sister, Carla; my niece, Clarissa; and my daughter, Jennica who are my heroes! They have been with me through everything, have seen me at my worst and are still my biggest fans. For my husband, Jamie, who supports and loves me and our children through every storm of life. I need his unfailing strength every day. For all my children: Kara (my witty first born who can climb a roof like a boss), Kyle (the most compassionate soul & best son, husband, and daddy around), Alec (who is super smart and working hard toward an industrial robotics certification), D'Andre (our strong-willed toddler who is now four years old and loves nothing more than playing outside, wearing cowboy boots, visiting our Florida house, and eating cheese), and Armoni (who is now a proud daddy and a bit more exhausted). I'm so honored to be called Momma by this crew! For Kyle's lovely wife, Stephanie, my sweet granddaughter, Embree, and adorable grandson Ryland who is almost walking at age 10 months. For Armoni's beautiful fiancé, Kaitlyn and sweet grandson Elijah who has the most gorgeous head of dark curls. Love my babies! For my brother, Rob, who unearths the coolest stories from the depths of history and loves words as much as I do. For my dad, Ray, who has been a constant pillar in my life and whose wisdom I carry in my heart. For my niece (and great nieces): Sabrina, Kinley, Molly and Jenah—some of the fiercest females on the planet whom I admire every day and would love to see more often! For my great nephews, Liam and Brayden, twins who never run out of things to say and who are about to graduate and launch into the great wide

Acknowledgments

world. For my nephew, Josh, who never ceases to amaze me with his resilience and hard work. For my forever-friend, Brian who has been incredibly loyal to me and my family! I'm beyond grateful for his friendship and willingness to help. For my dear friends and sisters-in-Christ whom I love and cherish daily. I can't even begin to name all of them, but they know who they are. For my former students with whom I've kept in touch—they are loved more than they know. For Mac Sandlin, truly one of the smartest people I am blessed to know. I could listen to him talk all day! And last, for my sweet dog, Max, who still chews on stuff but is trying to behave, and our new rescue dog, Scooter, another papillon-mix who has helped heal my heart.

Foreword

It is in the nature of poetry to break things apart. It is a language of impressions, but impressions presented in terse sharp lines rather than the gauzy pastels. Poems arise from a particular moment, a particular feeling, a particular insight, and they seek to make the particular into something universal —something that can be shared by the reader. In a poem, saying too much is often more dangerous than saying too little. Most of the page is blank space between the scattered lines of half sentences and fractured images– a million little pieces of truth laid side by side to form an image that gestures towards a wholeness beyond itself. The poet gathers up these impressions, packages them in words, and lays them out for us to see. This work of collecting and arranging is ubiquitous and yet goes mostly unnoticed and almost entirely unrewarded. As Guy Clark sang:

> There ain't no money in poetry
> That's what sets the poet free

And so, the tenacity of a poet like Arvilla Fee who keeps writing, keeps inviting us to see the world in fractured glimpses of her soul, is to be commended. In this collection, she explores the themes of brokenness and repair, pulling poems about war and poverty, division and isolation into "shapes akin to hope."

In an American style and a contemporary American context, she helps us see the naivety of our assumptions and the dangers of an unchanging "perfection pinned to a cork board." Her own experiences of motherhood, of the military, of care and concern for the

FOREWORD

dead and dying (the old and of the young, family and strangers, humans and animals), and of the presence of God inform the volume from beginning to end, as does her fierce hatred for cold.

Fee's is a scrappy poetry, a dandelion in a schoolyard of hard-packed dirt rather than a carefully tended rose from the garden. It fights its way up and shines out bright and yellow, and then it breaks apart and dances on the wind as it scatters until, at least, it finds a home in the hearts of her readers and begins to take root.

Mac Sandlin, PhD
Professor, Harding University

Preface

The happiest people are those who do the most for others. The most miserable are those who do the least.

—BOOKER T. WASHINGTON

It has been quite the journey writing *Mosaic: A Million Little Pieces* over the past year. In writing this third book (proceeded by *The Human Side* and *This Is Life*) I often found myself lamenting the bitter divisions in our country and around the world. It seems every time we turn on our televisions or catch new headlines on our phones, there are more wars, political upheaval, hatred, and turmoil. At times I despair over the cruelty and evil in human hearts. But then catastrophic events such as Hurricane Helene and Hurricane Milton occur, leaving millions with devastating losses, including loss of life, and I see a beautiful coming together, neighbors helping neighbors, strangers helping strangers without regard to race, color or creed. And it's *this* spirit of selfless, abundant giving that rekindles my hope for humankind. It's *this* kind of solidarity that makes me think perhaps our world isn't too broken after all—and that maybe, just maybe, we can be the kind of humans God wants us to be, if nowhere else, then at least in our own little corners of the world.

I hope you enjoy reading this book as much as I did writing it. I hope you find pieces of yourself embedded in sorrows, yesterdays, lives, natures, giggles, and triumphs. Perhaps you'll find just the piece you need—the one shard of broken glass you haven't touched

Preface

or thought about for years, and in this unexpected discovery, maybe you'll also find healing and peace. My prayer is that God opens our eyes and helps us see we are *all* part of the biggest mosaic every created.

Blessings to all,
Arvilla Fee

PIECES

scattered fragments
across hills and valleys,
deserts and plains,
what beauty lies in every
shade, every skin tone,
every hue of hair;
God's people huddled
on majestic planet earth,
each one made in His design,
each one carrying His breath;
we've wasted too much time
standing on opposite sides,
pretending we are not part
of the whole;
us, them, them, us—and yet
it's only through our solidarity,
only through our recognition
that we live on this round globe
as one mosaic under God's
Great Eye that we shall survive
as humankind.

PART I

A Million Sorrows

PART I | A MILLION SORROWS

AN ADAGE OF UNTRUTH

"All is fair in love and war"
~JOHN LYLY

spoken as if there are no rules to break,
as if love and war are both a free-for-all,

padded with excuses, immune from regrets,
but that's not the truth—not even a little;

all is not fair—not in love, not in war, both
have grave consequences, both have graves,

little white crosses scattered across fields,
across hearts cracked in dozens of places,

and it is upon these fallow grounds, where
people have fought, and bled, and died,

that we plant an adage of untruth, as a way
to placate ourselves, as a way to muster up

courage to reconstruct our lives into shapes
akin to hope.

ALL IS FAIR

He didn't ask for this—this land war;
nor did his father, his grandfather, or
his grandfather's father,
and yet—the scream of rockets,
plumes of fire and acrid smoke are as much
a part of his home as olive trees and ravens.
He thinks about his ancestors as he slinks
through a narrow alley beneath a bleak,
mid-waning moon and wonders how many
before him have cut down the same dark streets,
careful to avoid the bodies of the uncollected,
careful to remain unseen by prying eyes
as wildly desperate as his own.
Looking over his shoulder, he inches himself
towards a building, which, by some kind fate,
has remained standing—and within its limestone
walls lies something far more precious than gold,
a gift he will give to his children so he can soften
the hollow points of their cheeks.
He places three loaves of bread within the folds
of his overcoat and whispers, *God forgive me*
before closing the broken door.

PART I | *A MILLION SORROWS*

BUTTERFLY

You said you wanted
a butterfly;
so, I landed on your finger,
and you grinned;
I had no idea
you needed perfection
until you pinned me
to a cork board
for all the world to see.

THE CABIN CAT

Cool mist hangs over the valley—a gossamer blanket suspended just above the lush carpet of green. My therapist's voice hangs over my head: *practice the pause*—spiky words suspended just above my cerebral cortex. I tap my fingers against the well-worn wood, fidgety without my laptop. *Practice the pause.* That's what this week is supposed to be—one long pause. Guess that's what bawling in the staff bathroom will get you. I walk down two stubby steps into the dew-damp grass, *practicing the pause*. I bend down and run my fingers through dark green clover, dainty purple violets, and buttery dandelions, *practicing the pause*. Suddenly, I see a small movement from the corner of my eye. A thin gray tabby with luminous green eyes. She pauses. Meows. She's injured. I know the feeling. I squat down, hand extended. "Here, kitty, kitty." My voice is sing-song. Soothing. Saturated with calm. She comes to me, rubs her small sleek head against my open palm. Her ear is bleeding. I take her inside, bandage her up. We eat tuna for dinner. She pads around slowly. I pad around slowly. Like two old ladies in a care home — convalescing. *Pausing.* She falls asleep against my chest—our hearts beating in a syncopated rhythm. We will heal, she and I, from the inside out.

PART I | A MILLION SORROWS

DELIVERY PEOPLE

it's all in the presentation,
is it not?
in the way a newspaper
smacks the steps of a porch,
in the way four pizza boxes
precariously perched
on an outstretched hand
are passed to another,
in the way grocery bags
are placed near the front door,
coupons neatly tucked inside
for future savings,
in the way a doctor blinks
and steeples her fingers
to announce you have cancer,
in the way an officer stands
at the door, cap in hand,
his voice full of compassion
and regret—
I'm sorry about your loss.

MOSAIC

EMBEDDED

The mattress is concave,
hollowed out by your form,
and I sink into its empty depths
imagining I can still smell
the scent of your body wash,
that earthy bergamot—orange
with just a hint of spice.
I lie there some nights
enraged by the injustices
of the universe,
by places filled with sand
and wars not our own,
for whom were we fighting,
and for what?
There was no end game,
only flag-draped coffins
loaded into the backs
of airplanes.

PART I | *A MILLION SORROWS*

FADE TO BLACK

Languish is so close to anguish,
is it not? The way the two lie
side-by-side:
a wasting away,
the way my face contorts
in a concerted effort to hold back tears,
the way your hair comes out in clumps
and coats the inside of the shower,
the way I wipe it away with tissues.
Someone once asked me
if I'd rather see you shrink
or be snatched away in a car accident.
What can I say?
Neither?
I suppose this way, we get to say
all the things we never said;
a meandering goodbye
down the S-curve road
of treatments, vomit and fatigue.
Your hands are cold today;
I'll hold them in my own
and watch the valiant rise and fall
of your too-thin chest.

THE FALL OF US

I can see your breath
in the gray pre-dawn
and draw my robe tightly
around my frame;
spring is but a memory—
walks in the park, candles
on the dining room table;
summer, too, has passed,
cotton sheets grown cold
between two distant bodies;
I stare at golden leaves
now curling at the edges,
like your mouth's cruel grin;
tomorrow blooms will wilt
beneath fall's first bitter frost.

PART I | A MILLION SORROWS

THE GREATEST GRIEF

hollow—

an empty ribcage
rattles
with each sob,

breath catches
like legs
in brambles,

to love deeply,
even once,
and lose—

to mark a grave,
to scream,

to wake up alone,
to remember,

to name what ifs,
to want—

oh, the *ache* of wanting,

is perhaps
the greatest grief of all

I GREW THIN

the longer I stayed
with him
the thinner I grew,
not in body weight,
but
in substance,
in meaning—
diminished,
a mere mouse
of the self
I once knew,
so tiny
I no longer cast
a shadow

PART I | A MILLION SORROWS

INNOCENCE LOST

his cradled head
so sweet in the bed
blue eyes shut tight
it's a lullaby night
in light of the full Harvest moon

momma can't dream
that one day she'll scream
when a knock at the door
sends her knees to the floor
the baby she adored is now dead

he filled up his veins
then sat in the rain
a grownup young man
fresh out of plans
staring at hands he now hates

but his momma won't know
until that final blow
that the baby she cradled
just wasn't able
to table his demons tonight.

IN THE DARK

Oh, how we tried to reach out—
stretch our hands, grasp fingers,
tried to advise
        instruct
        scream;
I suppose we all turned blue
in the face,
and yet you chose
                wrong
again and again;
just couldn't stay away
from the edge
of self-destruction,
could you?
cocky, sure-footed,
you had it all under control,
didn't you?
Yet here you are—
blowing out
the last proffered candle;
so you can sit alone in the dark.

PART I | *A MILLION SORROWS*

THE LOVE AND LOSS OF A DOG

to give up grief
is to give up love,
and though I would like
to peel off the skin
of this searing pain
and find new skin
underneath,
would I be peeling away
the memories, too?
would I retract days spent,
side-by-side, thick as thieves,
the way your eyes followed me
as I walked across the room,
the way you would sigh
as you snuggled into my side,
the way your golden-brown eyes
peered into mine
as if I were the only human on earth,
the way your ears and tail would lift
every time I spoke your name;
the way you owned the sidewalk
when we took to the great outdoors,
the way you'd come running for treats,
the way you loved me with all your soul;
for someone to say you were "just a dog,"
only means they never had that kind of love
or that kind of loss.

MOSAIC

MEET ME BY THE RIVER

where the bank is muddy
and the water is cool
we'll go on pretending
our daughter's in school

we'll imagine her home
at the stroke of four
hungry for dinner
banging the door

we'll talk about boys
we'll talk about plans
she'll practice the tuba
she plays in the band

I won't watch your face
if you don't watch mine
we'll go on pretending
things are just fine

that day didn't happen
the freak with the gun
didn't unload a clip
and put a hole in our sun

we never got the call
that ended our world
we'll head back home,
see our little girl

meet me by the river
let it drown our tears;
what do we have left
but empty-nest years

MY SKIN FEELS SLICK WITH GRIEF

My skin feels slick with grief
as if someone has poured oil
over my head,
an unholy anointing;
I'm sorry for your loss
echoes
in the hollow chambers
of my mind.
I wonder how it's possible
to live in such a dichotomy,
forever suspended
between numbness and rage.
The well-wishers do mean well,
but to tell the story
over and over
leaves my tongue raw
and my lungs
begging for breath.

PART I | *A MILLION SORROWS*

NO WORDS

Unspeakable hurt—
the kind that curls you
into a fetal position,
leaves you to lie
in a darkened room
where even the bravest
ray of sun
dares not breathe
through closed blinds,
the kind of hurt
that dams up tears,
lodges them in the back
of the throat;
there's simply nothing
to say
and nowhere to go
except inside yourself.

OH, CHILD OF MINE

It was the doctor
who cut the cord,
your life blood,
your life bond to me.
It was she
who laid you
on my belly,
just above the womb
that once tucked you away
from the world.
But it was you
who cut the cord,
eighteen short years later,
cut the life blood,
cut the life bond to me.
It was you,
the untethered you,
who floated far beyond
the reach
of my now empty hands.

PART I | *A MILLION SORROWS*

PATTERNS

she will cover up the bruises
like she covers the gray
like she covers flowers
before a frost;
she will smile behind glasses
for better or worse
for the scales of justice
to remain blind;
she will keep going back
because of love
because of misspent days
of her youth.

PHANTOM PAIN

Like a severed limb—
they say you can't feel
the pain,
yet pain jitters like needles
stabbing the missing section
of your heart,
the chunk that broke off
and shattered like fine crystal
three seconds after the midnight call,
two seconds after the blood drained
from your face,
one second before time
cracked like a walnut
into then and now.

PART I | *A MILLION SORROWS*

RIBS

Washed up on the California shore,
a giant whale, beached,
with no resources of its own,
and then they came—the boats,
the nets, the scientists, each trying
to prod and poke and lift and lure
the whale back to safety;
but alas, no one could get him turned,
and he breathed his last;
one-by-one, the experts left,
and the crowds came to watch
a ribcage form in the absence of flesh.
I knew someone like the whale once,
beached—unable to help himself,
unwilling to be helped by others;
psychiatrists ran out of little pink pills,
therapists ran out of cool things to say,
so, left on his own, he breathed his last;
crowds gathered, tut-tutted the loss,
and the last thing we saw were his ribs.

MOSAIC

SHADOW GIRL

she's the one in the back row,
the one against the wall,
her back pressed into shadows;
she's the one who keeps her hood up,
the one not invited to parties,
the lone figure at a long lunch table;
she neither speaks nor is spoken to,
except for the occasional question
from her teachers;
she doesn't smile;
no one would notice if she did anyway;
she could be wearing yellow or brown;
it doesn't matter—
she blends in with the background,
an overlooked chameleon;
she has dreams—but no one
to whisper them to,
and she wonders. . .if dreams are never
spoken,
does anyone hear them fall?

PART I | A MILLION SORROWS

SOME THINGS WON'T BEAR THE WEIGHT OF WORDS

the unspeakable often remains
unspoken,
knit into bone marrow, muscles,
sinews, and ventricles of the heart—
lie-covered bruises,
an empty womb,
a lone cross at the side of the road,
a telegram of sincerest regret,
a bedroom turned mausoleum;
wracking sobs may cover the surface
of the red-raw pain, may dampen it,
allow for a modicum of functionality,
but the words—they just won't come,
and we swallow them down like glass
because to speak them is to fully realize
their weight—their weight far too great
for any chest to bear.

THE SUN ALWAYS RISES

down in a bayou a mother wails,
her cries rattle the cattails,
scatter the crawfish
and sink into the brackish water;
her womb once full is now empty,
as empty as the crib beside her bed,
but the sun cares not for empty cribs

in a hospital room a grandma breathes
her last breath—just ten minutes
before family arrives;
they hope they've said enough;
they hope she felt their love;
they wish they'd had more time,
but the sun cares not for time

in a city bar sits a lonely young man—
too drunk to leave, too broken to stay;
down to his last dollar,
he wonders where he'll find
another job to pay the bills;
down on your luck is a hard place to be,
but the sun cares not for luck

legs tangled in anxious sheets,
a young woman tries to still her breath;
she's made her bed with a monster,
and she blinks away salt-laden tears;
there will be new bruises today
and tomorrow and the day after that,
but the sun cares not for bruises

a shy young girl presses her back
against the gray walls of a high school,
hoping to remain invisible;
her mousy-brown hair doesn't bounce;
her tennis shoes are second-hand;
she carries a target on her back,
but the sun cares not for targets

Mosaic

THE THIN QUEST

pushing food
around on a plate,
creating artful empty spaces,
clothes that hide the hollows;
you laugh when required,
say all the right things,
nibble at the edges of carrots,
claim you had a big dinner
the night before,
well-placed collars cover clavicles,
those damn protrusions
everyone squawks about!
if you smile enough,
show up often enough,
be brave enough,
no one will know you bypass mirrors.

A TRAP OF YOUR OWN MAKING

The snap ricochets through the forest
like a thunderous gunshot.
I'm familiar with that sound,
iron-on-iron, a leg caught in between;
you've been trapped again, deceived
into thinking you could use one more time,
telling yourself it would be the *last* time,
that you'd get clean tomorrow, go to rehab.
No one will call me to free you, not anymore.
No one will ask me to coax you into relaxing
your snarled face with canines snapping
at the very hands that want to save you.
My phone will remain silent.
Someone else might come to your aid,
try to extrapolate the bleeding limb
from the jaws set by proficient hunters.
They knew what would lure you to the woods,
knew exactly what kind of bait
to place upon the loaded spring.
They were counting on your dependency,
on the collapse of a will far too weak to resist.
I cover my ears to mute the howls of fury;
there's nothing left for me to tame.

THE URNS WE CARRY

The funeral director,
with his slick-backed hair
and blue reading glasses
perched on the tip
of his sharp little nose,
solemnly announces
you can be placed
in more than one urn.
For a fee, you can sit
in dozens of urns—
at a cousin's or niece's
brother's or aunt's.
You need not be confined,
my love;
we can each carry
part of you in our hearts,
part of you back to our homes.

PART I | A MILLION SORROWS

THE WAY BACK

skin bruised deep plum

far away
from the life she'd imagined

she studies the card in her hand
Are you a victim of domestic violence?
You are not alone!

She'd never once wished to be a victim when she grew up. A firefighter. A professional chef. A flight attendant. Those had been some of her choices when her dreams were still fledgling fresh. People had written in her yearbook: *stay smart / you're the smartest person I know / you'll go places / go slay the future, girl*—and so on. But, for all the praise dedicated to her pre-frontal cortex, she'd made one wrong decision—she'd leapt before she looked.

He was charming at first—smiled, opened doors, caressed the small of her back. They wined and dined and wooed. He, the quintessential boyfriend. They became engaged three months later—married five months after that. Eight months. 243 days. She thought she knew him. And she did—until the first time he clenched his fists, sparks flaring in his gray-green eyes. *It's nothing*, she tried to tell him. *I ran into an old friend at the grocery store—not even someone I dated. We spoke, briefly, less than two minutes.* His response had been catastrophic, a mountain made out of a mole hill, if you will.

Mosaic

The first slap stunned her, sent her reeling. The second slap sent her to the floor. She may have screamed. She definitely cried. He apologized later. Sent her a dozen red roses. They moved on. And on. The next time would be the last time. Or the next time after that.

She flips the card over, fingers tracing the 10 digits over and over as if they are stars full of wishes.

PART I | *A MILLION SORROWS*

YOU KNOW

You never *really* know someone,
they say—but you do know;
you know when he slips out at night,
you hear the squeak of the hinges;
you know he'll be down on 5th street
and that there are dealers and users
congregating like brothers and sisters,
lighting up, blowing out, snorting;
you know he'll come back high;
he'll hug you and be sloppy-mouthed,
pupils dilated to three times their size;
you know that he'll deny everything
in the morning—make that noon-ish,
when he finally rises and breathes
unbrushed breath over your shoulder
while you are trying to eat your lunch;
you know, but don't say anything,
that he will not look for a job today,
nor any day after because that is work,
and he doesn't have time for that—
you know he simply lives
to keep his hands from shaking
to keep the demons off his back.

PART II

A Million Yesterdays

AFTER APOCALYPSE

imagine fingers combing
through the dust of us,
the debris of all we were,
like the city of Pompeii,
what would remain
to show the world
who we *were*,
among plastic bottles,
fast-food cartons,
tattered protest signs:
save our planet earth,
cubicles, eco cars,
cell phones shattered. . .
would they find the bones
of our division
would they dig up hate,
could our fragments
be magnified
between two glass slides,
a scientific testament
to what brought down
the human race?

THE AMERICAN BARN

I'm not sure why I loved that old barn so much,
but there was something about its disheveled state,
its faded American flag painted across the front
that warmed my insides—made me feel connected,
as if I was once part of the barn, as if I had gathered hay
from its rafters, had spent afternoons on a milking stool
reading epic novels and writing poetry.
And, as the barn began to lean like an arthritic old woman,
as boards began to split apart, I felt my heart split, too.
I was witness to its slow demolition; each time I passed
a few more boards were gone until one day—nothing.
They planted sunflowers where it once stood, beautiful
in their own way, I suppose, but woefully uninspiring.
They could never replace the weathered boards that held
time and history in every groove.

PART II | *A MILLION YESTERDAYS*

THE APPLE PEELER

Gram stood,
back slightly hunched,
brows furrowed
as though she were creating
a piece of art—
and I suppose she was,
as she deftly peeled away
the skin of the Honeycrisp apple,
not once taking anything away
from the white meat beneath;
I watched in utter amazement
as the peel grew longer and longer,
nearly translucent in the afternoon
light—this was my after-school snack,
one I looked forward to every day,
if for no other reason than to watch Gram
peel an entire apple without once
breaking the perfectly coiled strip.

AS THE CANDLE BURNS

the flame flickers,
bends with a puff of wind,
as if it can no longer carry
the weight of darkness;
she has burned through marriages,
and divorce, and children, sleepless
nights, weary footpaths on stairs;
she has burned through the death
of loved ones, great waxy tears
dripping inconsolably down her side;
she has burned through education
and career, upending, relocating,
growing pains of children now grown
—waiting patiently
for a reprieve,
a chance to breathe
a chance to shine,
with what wick and wax remain,
in the window of her own soul.

BAKER'S CABINET

If I close my eyes, I can still see Gram
standing in front of the baker's cabinet
wearing her red and white checked apron,
flattening a lump of dough with a wooden
rolling pin—a speck of flour on her nose;
she'd let me crimp the crust edges and add
the ripe-red summer strawberries, sweet
enough to eat without a drop of sugar;
how many times had I opened drawers
and doors to put things away, to get things
out, standing on tiptoes to reach shelves
taller than my gangly ten-year-old self?
Gram is long gone, but the baker's cabinet
remains, still in the same place in her kitchen;
it would be unwieldy to move, and yet—
if it *could* be moved, if my mother asked me
if I wanted it—would I take it? Or would I raise
my eyes to heaven and beg Gram to forgive me
for my too-modern kitchen,
for rushing to the supermarket
to buy a store-made pie?

MOSAIC

BEGINNINGS TRIOLET

We bought a hut with an ocean view
on the rocky cliffs of Maine;
when funds were low, and love was new,
we bought a hut with an ocean view.
With pieces of me and pieces of you,
(I liked yellow, you liked blue);
we blended separate lives.
We bought a hut with an ocean view
on the rocky cliffs of Maine.

A BETRAYAL OF BONES

The creak and squeak
of calcium sticks,

the rising, the sitting, the bending,
as if they have not supported my frame

for almost eighty years,
as if they have forgotten their history,

their original fortitude
that allowed a girl to climb apple trees.

THE BREATH

of memories
fog my mind;
I can't see through the pane.
I can't see through the pain.

But I trace my fingers
in the condensation
and make a lopsided heart,

a heart that once held
the whole of you,
unbroken by tragedy,

that split second in time
that divided then and now
and left me unprepared

to navigate a world
never quite warm enough.

PART II | *A MILLION YESTERDAYS*

CLEMENTINE STOCKINGS

logs frizzle in the fire
stockings hang   empty
limp little things without feet
waiting for providence

the jolly man with belly and pipe
is but a fairy tale unraveling
around the loosening threads
of children's minds

but the slight woman,
arthritic fingers   aching
slips pieces of the sun
into each hopeful toe.

CRAWDADS AND BOLOGNA

to be little again
to think that catching crawdads
and wading in the creek
is as near to heaven
as any statued saint

to be skinny again
to eat bologna sandwiches
on bread so fresh
it sticks to the roof
of your mouth

to be free again
and run like antelope
across a field of wildflowers
with the sinking sun
your only clock

to be alive again
in spirit, in body
not a joint out of place
grinning with beautiful teeth,
hair tousled like a robin's nest

PART II | A MILLION YESTERDAYS

to have dreams again
to imagine being anything
you want to be—
never considering impossible,
holding the world in your hands

MOSAIC

A DIVISION OF GOODS

When grandma passed
oh, you should have seen
how the children, grandchildren,
cousins, aunts and uncles
fought over her possessions.

She wasn't rich by any means,
but she had stuff—you know,
collectibles, antiques, pictures,
a set of china (which may have
been worth something).

But the way they carried on,
well, you would have thought
they stood to gain millions,
and it soon became a contest
about whom was the closest,

who knew her best, who she'd
want to have this thing or that,
and I let them squabble
because all I wanted was one
teaspoon, the one she'd used

PART II | A MILLION YESTERDAYS

every day to stir her hot tea,
the silver one with a flat handle,
the one she would lick remnants
of honey from before setting it
beside her cup on a saucer.

So, I took that one spoon;
I don't think anyone noticed.
Today I stir my tea, savor the
honey, and she's sitting here,
grinning like the Cheshire Cat.

MOSAIC

DUST TO DUST

we all see them—tiny dust motes
floating in the air against the backdrop
of sunbeams
filtered   through smudged panes;
they hover, as if hoping to be noticed,
and perhaps they do want to be seen
in all their glory, specks from the dead,
                look at me,
look at what I've become,
after the decay, after worms have had
their fill, it's me you see—
a shimmery mote,
just before I fall to the table,
the floor, that picture frame on the sill,
just before you gather me up
in your microfiber cloth
and shake me out   on the porch

PART II | A MILLION YESTERDAYS

FOREVER EIGHTEEN

a click—a moment,
captured in less than a second
but preserved like strawberry jam
in the time capsule of digital prints,
the way the light refracted
around the summer-green leaves,
the way a cigarette sat, cockeyed
above his left ear,
the jaunty grin in a suntanned face,
the recklessness of his hiking boot
propped against the tire of his Jeep,
the click—a moment
that turned time into eternity,
that made him ageless,
forever sealed in memories.

THE GAP

pauses between conversations
stretched like a day-old yawn,
the television grew louder,
unlit candles collected dust
on the dining room table;
neither of us said grace;

and so began the building
of your palisade, each wooden stake
driven into the ground with precision,
intended to keep me out;
the thud thud thud of your mallet
hammered against my rib cage

at first, I peered over the top;
I could see you if I stood on tiptoe,
but my toes grew weary,
weighted as they were by my soul;
so, I packed a bag, slipped through
a crack and left you to your fortress.

PART II | A MILLION YESTERDAYS

GENETICS

didn't allow me beautiful hands
but the worn, road-map hands
of my mother
and grandmother,
and I suspect the mothers
and mothers before her—
not a single hand model
among them
but workers of the soil,
the kitchen,
the bath and laundry,
menders of clothes,
canners of vegetables,
cotton pickers,
cow milkers,
hair braiders,
hands meant for daily toil,
washed often in harsh soap,
dried on the nearest towel
or on the folds of fabric
clinging to the bone-sturdy bodies
of women meant to bear children
and pass down capable hands
to their daughters.

THE GOLDEN YOUNG

a delicate, salty mist covers my arms;
it's just-right-warm on the beach,
a light breeze blowing in from the east,
fanning my hair around my neck;
I walk quickly, arms pumping—just enough
to be called power walking;
I can't help but notice the younger crowd—
achingly, *exquisitely* beautiful;
I would say, post-menopause, that I miss my abs,
but truth is, I never had them,
at least I don't think so.
I wonder what they see when they look at me,
a late-fifties woman wearing a t-shirt, shorts
and baseball cap.
Actually, they probably don't see me at all.
They are sheltered, for now—
        sanguine
in their sun-kissed bodies, decades away
from skin cancer screenings and wrinkles.

PART II | *A MILLION YESTERDAYS*

THE GRUDGE

I hold the grudge against my chest,
hardened, rough as rock;

some say time can heal all wounds,
but they don't watch the clock.

Lady Justice might not witness
every travesty—

knives cut deepest in the back,
a fall with gravity.

But karma often comes around
in its own inventive ways;

the flower with the proudest bloom
still ends up in decay.

MOSAIC

THE HANDS THAT HELD

a jar of peaches
freshly canned,

ribbons braided
into hair,

a painted canvas
(her Van Gogh),

flowers planted
every spring—

can no longer hold
        anything,

can no longer make sense
        of the world,

but sit idly in her lap
        like a paper-thin map

of roads no longer traveled.

PART II | A MILLION YESTERDAYS

IF YOU DECIDE TO GO

Take that blue lamp I never liked,
the yard-sale bicycle with one wheel
you were always (never) going to fix,
that framed piece of art—
which still doesn't look like a pineapple;
take the coffee pot that leaks,
the brown rug that never stays in place,
the ceramic duck you bought in Mexico;
take your fair-prize goldfish—I swear
that idiot will outlive us both;
take your golf shorts and that raggedy
Rolling Stones t-shirt shirt I like to wear
on Saturdays,
take the cinnamon toothpaste,
which is too hot anyway
and that ridiculous dancing mouse
with the crooked Santa hat;
take your pinball machine—
I'll still have the highest score;
just leave me be,
leave the tissues on the nightstand,
the take-out menus in the drawer,
leave my vintage wine glass
we picked up in Rome.

Mosaic

I WISH YOU COULD'VE STAYED

a little longer,
just enough
for one more meal
for one more terrible joke
only funny because it was so terrible,
for one more cup of tea
although we'd drunk three already
    for one more walk around the block
    for one more who-done-it guess
during that Friday night crime show
    for one more wake up
    for one more lie down
    for one more moment
we thought we had left

PART II | *A MILLION YESTERDAYS*

KANSAS 1935

the wind blows through the cracks—
cracks in the doors, the floors,
cracks around the window sills;
it wails like an injured animal,
feral, enraged—
looking for a way in, a way out,
and I rock in the rocker
in this tar-paper shack,
stopping only to slug down
a half bottle of whiskey
and curse the drought
which cursed the prairie
which left me with nothing
but a bowl full of dust

MOSAIC

THE KEEPING ROOM

a bone china teapot
with tiny blue roses,
a lace doily
which covers a scratch
on the oak side table,
three paperbacks,
(all mystery thrillers)
one still has a bookmark
on page 119,
house slippers
formed over time
to the exact shape
of her size 6 feet,
a threadbare quilt,
its ocean blues faded
to a muted gray,
the cuckoo clock
that always kept time
ten minutes ahead,
the garden statue
of a bunny
that never quite made it
to the garden;
the room had kept
everything
but her.

PART II | A MILLION YESTERDAYS

THE LAST DRIVE-IN MOVIE THEATER

those summer nights, ripe with humidity
humming with mosquitos
thrumming with hormones
the truck parked backwards
tailgate facing the king-sized screen,
music playing through tinny speakers
the smell of popcorn, pretzels and fake cheese
wafting over the grassy lot stacked twenty deep
with convertibles, old beaters, even a tractor
or two—tanned arms and legs hanging out
of doors and windows, cigarette smoke
drifting around heads like Caesar's laurel,
those were the nights slick with sweat,
flush with freedom

LEFTOVERS

VW van, decked out
in peace and love,
circa 1968,
rusted in places,
eaten through
like moth-riddled clothes,
outfitted
with new retro hippies:
unwashed dreadlock hair,
unapologetic polyester,
headbands and a faint,
sickening-sweet scent
that wafts across the campground
beneath a star-spattered sky;
we fall asleep to the strum
of acoustic guitars
and smoke-gutted voices
rasping *Hey Jude*.

PART II | A MILLION YESTERDAYS

LOST LIBRARIES

I inhale the scent of pages pressed into book
spines, real ink-on-paper with no chargers,

rows and rows of books stretched long-ways,
planted by gifted farmers of the literary world,

seeds upon seeds of imagination and truth
and memories that sprouted to life under suns

of press and printers. I understand the three
aged men who park themselves in cushy chairs

of the periodical section each day, gray-haired
and a tad bit creased around plump edges;

they lift the newspapers as if news comes
from no other source, as if everything worth

knowing is now resting on their black-smudged
fingers. And perhaps it is. Perhaps those pages

hold all we need to know, and the book I clutch
to my chest contains a virgin world undefiled
by progress.

OUR CUP OF COFFEE

We were like a fine cup of gourmet coffee,
    bold
        rich
            bursting with flavor,
complimenting each other with just-right
amounts of sugar and cream,
an aromatic dream—
but then we forgot to drink it,
misplaced our cup somewhere,
and we cooled

over time,
you and I became undrinkable.

PASSED DOWN

It lies in my palm,
a small square card
from beyond the grave,
hand-scripted with broad
bold strokes of a pen,
as confident as the woman
who'd written the words:
a cup of this,
a teaspoon of that,
a dash of salt, of course…
my eyes scan the card
again and again,
a smudge of butter,
a dot of flour on a corner
bent with time and age.
The entire image blurs
like an abstract painting
as tears fill my vision—
my gram's secret recipe
for apple dumpling cake;
she'd passed it down
to me,
with a classic red lipstick
kiss on the back.

MOSAIC

REMEMBERING I DON'T REMEMBER

There are days when I'm lucid;
I heard my nurse use that word,
and I kind of like it—*lucid*.
That means I remember my name,
where I am,
the names of the children
who visit me.
It's those lucid days
that I also remember I forget things,
when a misty fog drapes over my brain
and blocks out the simplest things—
like what I had for breakfast.
The lucid days also scare me
because I don't know how long they'll last,
how long I'll look into my daughter's blue eyes
and remember how she once fell out of a tree
and got a cut just above her left eyebrow,
or remember the names of all five grandchildren
or that I simply adore the color yellow.
I wonder if it would be better to remain in the fog,
tucked away behind the gray matter that holds
my age-old storybook,
but, no, I think not.
My eyes grow heavy,
and I mutter to myself as I begin to doze,
stay lucid, stay lucid, stay lucid.

REVERSAL OF ROLES

To see a shrunken man
curved into a chair
sears my heart
with a grown up brand
I'm not prepared to bear;
this man, my dad,
once a bulldozer,
pushing earth and sky
in that willful way of his,
now uses a shoehorn
to coax his heels
inside his walking shoes;
I bite my tongue
to keep from stepping
on his remaining pride
and pretend I'm OK
as I watch him walk outside
and climb (stiffly) into his car
and drive himself to the store.
I know he must keep up
appearances, and he will say,
I'm fine
until the angels seal his lips.

MOSAIC

THERE'S A MEADOW

There's a meadow beyond the back pasture
of my grandpa's old farm, and when I was a city
kid, it scared me—that vast openness brimming
with nothing but wildflowers, insects, and birds.

Grandpa often took me there to read and think.
The reading I didn't mind, but I had no idea what
to think. "Relax your mind, Jenny Bell," he'd say.

And so we'd lie there on his red-checkered blanket,
staring at the endless expanse of sky, making shapes
out of the cottony clouds, pieces of grass between

our teeth. The hum of insects would make me drowsy,
but I'd stay awake. Grandpa would eventually tell me
his thoughts, mostly about how to invent new tractors

or what to name the new calves that were nearly born.
One time, I surprised myself by telling him about middle
school and how I didn't like Harvey Winters because he

stuck gum on people's seats and made fun of the freckles
on my nose. "Why do you suppose he does that?" Grandpa
asked. That's where all the thinking came in—"I suppose

it's because his mama is dead, and he doesn't have a good
daddy," I said. Grandpa made an umm hmm noise, but didn't
add anything. He let me think some more. Over the years,

PART II | *A MILLION YESTERDAYS*

Grandpa and I shared lots of thinking time, and nearly every one ended with—*why do you suppose*. Grandpa died when I was twenty-three, right after I graduated with a psychology

degree. But every now and then, I leave my office and return to the farm. I lie down in that back meadow, a blade of grass between my teeth, and I talk to Grandpa just like I used to.

When I'm puzzling things out in life, I hear his voice, *Why do you suppose*? And I find my answers floating among clouds shaped like lions while a butterfly rests on my chest.

TOO YOUNG TO KNOW

There's a thrashing near the fence,
and my heart jumps, alert to danger.

But then I spot her, a beautiful fawn
just losing her spots, tangled in wire.

I can see the whites of her eyes
as I approach with cutting shears

and speak the common language
of compassion for a hurting soul.

I carefully snip her back legs free,
and as she bounds toward the trees,

I can't help but wish someone
had cut me lose when I was young

and too dumb to avoid fences.

PART II | A MILLION YESTERDAYS

UNMENDED

The cold March air burrows into my bones. Even through thick gloves, my hands have grown cold. Daylight is fading, and I tell myself, just one more section of repairs. Lost in thoughts of hot tea and house slippers, I nearly jump out of my skin at the sound of thrashing somewhere ahead where the fence nears the tree line. I suck in a breath as I see a young doe—her neck caught in strands of broken barbed wire. As I approach, her eyes roll wildly, and I speak to her as though she were a child—like I used to speak to my daughter years ago, "It's okay. Don't be afraid." Her body quivers, and I slowly approach with wire cutters. Snip. Snip. Now free, I expect her to bolt, but she gently nudges my cheek before vanishing into the forest. Perhaps she has forgiven me for the human encroachment and pricks of pain.

on chipped Formica

letters lie unopened
return to sender

perhaps someday
I will touch the freckled nose
of my daughter

Mosaic

WE USED TO

talk for hours,
bump shoulders
in a postage-stamp kitchen,
take long walks around the lake,
fancy ourselves first-rate detectives
as we solved every crime show on TV,
but now we're silent as we pass
in a kitchen with granite tops;
the lake is distant memory,
the TV, distant noise;
we can't solve
our crimes.

PART II | A MILLION YESTERDAYS

WHEN MY METABOLISM WAS YOUNG

sun-tanned legs pumping,
flinging dirt and gravel
as the supper bell rang—
the best sound in the world,
and I would dig into my plate
with fork and knife and spoon,
meatloaf smothered in gravy,
potatoes smothered the same,
yeast rolls fresh from the oven,
green beans with bacon,
corn-on-the-cob dripping butter;
those were the days of eating
for the pure satisfaction
of a contented belly—full
and round and warm,
when calories vanished
into thin air
as I rode my bike up and down
grass-green hills,
made mud pies with my brother,
waded the creek,
and chased fireflies,
my face flushed with life.

WORN AROUND THE EDGES

He hands her a bunch
of yesterday's carnations,

slightly wilted,
marked 50% off;

she hands him
a slightly wilted smile.

YOU ONCE TOLD ME I
WAS BEAUTIFUL

in the spring
when stems were new,
blossoms bright
against the mid-March sun;

we blazed together
during summer,
blown by tipsy winds,
electrified by stars;

you still held me
as dew tipped the grass
in frosted-silver droplets,
and gold hung from my arms;

but then the leaves fell,
as did the temperature,
as did your eyes, your smile;

I suppose you shivered
at the sight of naked branches,
a strange fragility,

but darling, did you not know
that a new spring would come,
that I would bloom again,
thrusting through crusted earth;

Mosaic

    you see I am a perennial,
    back every year, lovely, fresh—
    she is just an annual
    and will be gone by season's end.

PART III

A Million Lives

PART III | A MILLION LIVES

THE 1930S AUNTIE BRIGADE

There was no getting by with anything
on 42nd Street—no sneaking out late,
no skipping school, no throwing rocks,
no swearing, no fist fights, no stealing,
not with the three aunties planted
like cathedral gargoyles on the front steps
of the crumbling brick apartment complex.
They knew the names of every resident
from top to bottom and had designated
themselves *keepers of the block.*
Adorned in flowered house dresses,
bright colors clashing like spilled paint,
us kids gave them a pretty wide berth,
as they were known to carry spatulas
and issue swift attitude adjustments
with a smack to the back of the head.
Didn't do any good to duck, as they would
chase us down the block, screeching
in Italian: Ti farò entrare il buon senso—
I didn't know much Italian, but even I
understood, *I will beat sense into you*!
Half of me lived in fear of them,
but the other half of me lived in awe,
as they were also known to slip an apple
to a hungry boy or discover a pair of shoes
once wore by their children (now grown)
to pass along to those of us stuffing
newspapers to cover holes in our soles—

Mosaic

but the one thing I remembered most,
the thing that has carried me through
adulthood, is something the aunties
said to me every day my pop was away
looking for work: il sole sorgerà domani
    the sun will rise tomorrow
and they were right; it always has.

PART III | *A MILLION LIVES*

AGING OUT

Home to home,
a trash bag full
of junk:
teddy bears
she'll never hold,
a snow globe
without snow,
a paper calendar
full of X marks;
the system will cut
the cord
and hand her
to the world,
red-faced and screaming,
the minute
she turns eighteen.

THE BALLAD OF RETURNING SOLDIERS

If you look into my eyes
you might see a shade of blue;
I hope you notice in your hurry
that I still shed tears too.

Just because I've fought in wars
doesn't mean I'm granted grace;
turns out when they send you home
you can lose your safest space.

Dead men often come a-knocking,
pounding on the door of dreams;
when I'm face-down on the hardwood,
I can hear their fetid screams.

I know you probably look at me,
a grizzly man with cardboard sign
and entertain a fleeting thought
before I vanish from your mind.

I truly cannot cast the blame,
for I was once like you,
things to do, things to see;
the day was mine to choose.

PART III | A MILLION LIVES

I guess the hardest part of all
is knowing I'm still here
while all others have forgotten
as though I have disappeared.

BARTENDER

her hands are rough, red
too much soapy water
too many dipped beer mugs,
but they have a certain elegance,
a way of moving like butterflies,
swiftly lighting from mug to tap,
grabbing bottles, swiping the counter
with a clean white cloth;
she's thin with long, dark hair,
a lotus tattoo on her shoulder
where her black tank exposes skin;
her bright blue eyes are alert,
in tune with every movement
around her, at constant attention
to meet the customers' needs,
and yet there are faint purple shadows
resting like little half-moons just beneath,
and her bright smile belies the ache
in her back.

PART III | *A MILLION LIVES*

THE BLIND MAN'S NOSE

The corner diner
sits just two blocks
from his home,
easily walked
with his white pole
and the chirping signals;
he enters the narrow room
      inhales:
he's here, the construction man
who smells of concrete dust
and freshly cut lumber;
she's here, the teacher
who smells of books
and students' anxiety;
the toddler and mother are here,
carrying the scent of diapers,
baby shampoo and fretting;
he waits—gently sniffing;
ah, there she is,
the woman who smells of lilacs
and Tuscany suns,
the one who pats his hand
and tells him good morning.

COLD SHOULDER

It was her way—
tight-lipped,
eyes staring
into the distance,
back rigid
as an ironing board;
he'd asked her
what was wrong,
waited—listened
to the dripping faucet,
a rogue cricket
chirping from a corner
of the narrow kitchen,
but he knew no answer
would come
from those dead-bolt lips;
it was her way,
arms folded
across her chest,
a cauldron of thoughts
locked inside
her stubborn head.

PART III | *A MILLION LIVES*

DEAR DAUGHTER

You are my true North,
that steady star
always on the horizon,
fixed,
sure.
You are my core,
my balance,
my upright,
uncollapsible.
You are my rock,
not the burden kind,
but the one I look at
over and over,
solid,
there.
You are my legacy,
an extension of my life,
the mirror of my eyes,
the continued beating
of my heart.
You are my daughter,
the best part of me.

DEAR JOHN DONNE

You once said *No man is an island,*
but I wonder, John, is that really true?
What about the man who lives alone,
no family, no friends, no one knows
he's dead for five days—and then only
by the scent of his cloying decay.
And what about the girl in the cafeteria?
The one eating alone, her tray floating
on the brown sea of an empty table,
her tears washed up on distant shores?
And what about the old man who sits
staring vacantly out smudgy windows
in a nursing home, his children too busy
with lives of their own—or perhaps he
no longer remembers them?
And what about the widow who picks
through sepia photos, reliving her days
as a bride as she sips her tea and eats
a meal made for one.

PART III | *A MILLION LIVES*

DONATION TUESDAYS

Eyes downcast,
the middle-aged woman
with unkempt hair
and baggy trousers
shuffles forward
in the designated line.
She extends her hand,
and I place the loops
of the white plastic bag
filled with canned goods
across her open fingers.
She glances up,
and something akin to fire
flashes in the depths
of her dark blue eyes;
I wasn't always like this,
she says in a husky voice.
Then shuffles away,
her untied shoelaces
gently tapping the tiles.

Mosaic

EVERYONE SMILES BUT THE CLOWN

> *"Because no retreat from the world
> can mask what is in your face."*
> —Gregory Maguire, Wicked

Always part of the circus,
juggling a thousand pins
beneath the big top.

White-hot spotlights cast
a golden glow upon a face blurred
beneath charisma and paint.

The audience roars as he trips over
his too-big feet. He's up in an instant,
bowing, enticing the crowd to eat

his antics like popcorn. They don't see
sweat circles under his arms, don't feel
the jagged edges of his scarred heart.

He's a performer—and has the cash
to prove it, but as the lights go down,
and the laughter fades, and he slips

like a phantom into his dressing room,
he alone can battle the demons
behind the looking glass.

PART III | A MILLION LIVES

FINAL SYMPHONY

He closes his eyes
letting notes from the cellos
wash over him
like warm summer rain,
but in his mind,
he still sees her—
shriveled like an apple
lain too long on the ground,
spotted with too many trips
around the sun,
bedridden.
His mother.
He should be with her.
He knows this,
but the orchestra director
had begged him to come,
to critique his last performance
before retirement.
So, he had.
Now he sifts through
the light-footed flutes,
the deep-throated bassoons,
marking comments
in his little black book;
his mother takes her last breath
at home.

THE HONEYBEE BOX

She moved like a ghost
through the fog-filled meadow,
hat and veil covering her head,
I would make the sign of the cross
as we passed the graves of the dead.
This aunt was a mystery to me;
she only conversed with the bees.

Her sister mentioned
a defect in her brain
a baffling mishap at birth,
but even in her strange silence,
she seemed at home with the earth.
She was like sunshine to me;
I thought it lovely she talked to bees.

She'd let me follow
when she gathered honey;
I'd wear my own special suit,
with gloves bound around each wrist
and my oldest pair of black boots;
she always said thank you and please
to the sweet swarm of golden-brown bees.

I'd stand aside as she smoked the hive
listening to her low melody,
a secret language no one else knew;
a love song just for the bees.

PART III | A MILLION LIVES

THE KINDNESS EXPERIMENT

It's late-September; the kids are restless,
too many bodies and too much sunshine
and high temps to be considered fall;
so, I try something new, something to shift
their attention away from the stifling air
and the drudgery of settling into routines.

*We are going to do a kindness experiment,
I announce to the class. Each day, you will
complete one act of kindness for someone
in this school, preferably someone you don't
already know.* I hear groans, see actual panic
written on a few frowning faces.

But I plow ahead, *It can be something small:
picking up something someone dropped,
allowing someone to go in front of you in the
lunch line, offering to carry a lunch tray. . .you
get it, right? And write down the kind deeds
in a journal. I'll collect them in two weeks.*

The bell rings, there are shuffles, a few more
groans, but I feel a shift in energy—one student
holds the door open for another, another says,
hey, did you drop this? and picks up a pencil.
I smile to myself to see the experiment already
in motion—ripples in a pond that I hope will grow.

MOSAIC

Two weeks later, I ask for volunteers to read from their *Acts of Kindness Journals*, and I am stunned into silence, tears rolling down my cheeks. Dozens of students rise, and I'm suddenly clutching about twenty-five tissues. *These kids*, I think. *These are* my *generous, kind, loving kids*!

LIGHT FROM WITHIN

I pick up an old paperback,
absently thumbing its pages
until a faded photograph
flutters to the floor,
making me draw a sharp breath.
Gramp's old lighthouse.
I gently stroke the worn edges,
and I'm in Maine, a kid again.
I can feel the clammy chill,
the sting of salt in my nose,
the unforgiving slap of concrete
beneath my battered boots.
Mom never understood
how Gramps could live there
on that God-forsaken piece of land
perched like a hawk above the sea.
But I understood. Gramps was light.
He was polish, and glass, and steel,
fresh white paint, quilts, a trundle
bed with feather pillows. And me—
I was his constant shadow, begging
him to teach me the language of ships.
It was only when his white beard
grew long, and my legs grew longer
—and arthritis curled his fingers
while I curled my eyelashes
that I began to feel a sense of loss,
a growing-up-ness I could not escape.

MOSAIC

But when I mentioned it to him,
Gramps had patted my knee and said,
Childhoods are never lost,
just sometimes misplaced.

PART III | A MILLION LIVES

MAMA AND PAPA'S DANCE

A new record spun on the player,
round and round, round and round
while Papa waltzed Mama across
our citrine-yellow carpet.

I could see them from my perch
in the little window that divided
the living room from kitchen,
my feet dangling over the edge.

Mama threw her head back
and laughed; Papa dipped her
like one does an ice cream cone
in chocolate shell coating.

I loved it all—the Beatles,
the stack of 45s, the floral couch,
Mama's skirt swishing just below
her knees, Papa's overalls.

But it couldn't last, could it—not
my childhood, not their dancing
because bills come due, more
babies come due, nerves frayed,

MOSAIC

and tempers flared. Papa drank,
Mama cried; her hands grew red
from doing other people's laundry,
just to keep collectors off the porch.

Our olive-green fridge rarely held
enough milk; it was hard to come by,
and the government only issued
so much cheese and bread.

Papa stopped smiling, worry lines
replacing smile lines, and Mama
stashed her dresses in the closet
and started wearing pants.

PART III | *A MILLION LIVES*

MY FATHER, THE LONELY MECHANIC

his cuticles bear crescent moons
of unwashable grease,
days spent beneath the hoods
of cars, digging into their bowels,
searching for complicated answers
to the knock, the ping, the whine,
living from paycheck-to-paycheck,
coming home late—too tired
to crack a joke or smile,
only enough energy left to crack
open a bottle and swig its contents
in long gulps down a throat
that buried its hum in the ribs
of my mother the day cancer
lifted her out of her body and left us
with a shell   of all we'd ever been

MOSAIC

NEURODIVERGENT PROCESSING

people pressing,
elbows and shoulders
jockeying for position;
there are so many,
too many,
and suddenly, I can't breathe,
the air is hot and humid
with a million moving lips,
and there are lights everywhere,
florescent overhead,
luminescent signs saying open,
saying 50% off sale,
saying buy one get one free,
and the noise rises
up, up, up to the vaulted ceilings,
creating a ringing in my ears,
so many voices and sounds,
chatter, laughter,
the squeak of tennis shoes,
the man at a kiosk
asking if I want to try a sample,
a sample of what, I don't know;
I can't look at him,
can't think, can't hear;
I'm drowning in a sensory pool,
the water closing in over my head,
the smell of fish and pizza and tacos
nearly making me ill;

PART III | *A MILLION LIVES*

I strip off my jacket
as if the release of this one layer
will somehow free my body, my mind,
but it doesn't—so, I walk outside,
leaving the crescendo behind
and stand, eyes closed, in the muted air.

ONCE AROUND THE BLOCK

Lenny's eyes sag, his chin sags;
he's just one sad sack of bones
bound to a wheelchair.
Bored—bordering on depression.
No family. No visitors. Stuck.
Come on, Lenny, I say.
He lifts bushy gray eyebrows,
casting me a look of reproach,
as if I'm taking him to Bingo.
But as soon as I key in my code
making the front doors whoosh open,
Lenny grins and fist pumps the air.
I start slowly, but Lenny calls me Gramps,
so, I push faster, cringing as we hit the cracks.
Get in the road, Lenny barks. *It's smoother!*
I check for cars then take off, almost at a jog!
Lenny squeals and holds up his hands
like he's riding a roller coaster.
A car comes up behind us, and I start to move,
but Lenny yells that we have the right-of-way.
The driver pulls up beside us, grinning and waving.
Then another car comes along, then another.
They all drive by slowly, honking and cheering
like we're in a parade and Lenny has won Fair King.
Back at the building, Lenny's lean face is flushed,
and his white hair is standing up in little tufts.
That was the best road trip ever! Lenny says.
I cannot agree more.

PART III | *A MILLION LIVES*

POLISHING STARS

Hey, Teach, just letting you know,
I can't write.

I smile. I've heard this before;
it's English class after all.

We'll see about that, I say.
Days later, I hand back the essays;

his paper has an A and a large
smiley face drawn at the top,

and I've written—*and you told me*
you couldn't write!

The million-watt smile on his face is
priceless; *How did I get an A*, he asks.

Because you did exactly what you
were asked to do, I say.

He grins again and hugs his paper.
I've just polished another star.

*Thank you Aaron Pritchard for this inspiration. May you always shine!

RECALL OF A SOLDIER

Except for the missing leg,
you'd never know about the bomb,
how I catapulted through the air,
thinking I would never land.
You'd never know about the months
I spent in rehab—
or about this freak prosthetic
I'm still trying to figure out.
Except for the twitch in my jaw,
you'd never see the film loop
in my brain, how it keeps playing
the same frames: explosion, bodies,
the red-soaked sand.
Except for my night sweats
and hands grasping for my gun
as I sit bolt upright in bed,
you'd never know the enemy
is approaching; he never goes away.
And when you say, "Thank you
for your service," I know
what you really mean,
"Thank you for the stories
I'll never have to tell."

PART III | A MILLION LIVES

RUNNER

legs stretched   long, lanky—
sweat drawing circles under armpits,
a heart beats, beats, beats, beats
in rhythm to trainers slapping pavement.
She's going somewhere;
happiness lies
just over the next hill,
or is it the one after that?
The hills all look alike,
that row of pines no different
than the last,
but she picks up speed,
forges ahead;
one day she will outrun
herself.

SECRET FAITH

I step into what was once
a clandestine Catholic church
(1581, Amsterdam)
and try to imagine the scene—

parishioners breaking the law,
slipping quietly into pews
to worship their banned God
behind black windowpanes,

perhaps I am sitting
in the same place
another woman sat;
are her tearstains on the floor?

did she light a candle;
did she bring her children here;
did they whisper prayers;
did she escape a bitter fate?

a shiver runs through me,
as though I've stepped
over someone's grave;
I light a candle for the ghosts.

PART III | A MILLION LIVES

SEND IT

Send it, my therapist says.
Send the letter.
I look down at the rumpled envelope
in my lap, the one that contains
two sheets of paper, the thirteenth draft,
the one I'd finally deemed worthy to keep,
but now, I'm not so sure;
did I say enough to my absent father,
did I tell him, in no uncertain terms,
how I felt when he walked away
just after my tenth birthday?
How it felt watching his back disappear
around a bend in the lane;
did I tell him how I missed fishing with him
on the docks, him showing me how to cast
the line, just so, him patting my back
when I caught a big one, a small one,
even when I threw one back in the lake?
Did I tell him how I missed the smell
of his woodsy soap and cherry tobacco,
how I sniffed and sniffed the two ragged shirts
he'd left behind like parentheses
in an otherwise empty drawer?
Perhaps I *should* send the letter,
and perhaps, just perhaps, he will open it,
and his face will grow wet with great salty tears
for the red-haired girl with two braided pigtails
who stood at the open screen door asking,
Why, Daddy? Why?

SPANISH MOSS CHRONICLES

She sits among the pines and palmettos,
a canopy of Spanish moss draped overhead.
She knows how she looks—a daft old woman
dressed in a sleeveless butter-yellow dress,
white curls tied back in a knotted bandana.
But frankly, she doesn't care; she relishes
the hot, moist air that gives life to the forest.
If anyone were to stop and ask, she'd tell them
to sit with her and listen to stories of the dead,
parents, grandparents, their parents—as told
through the kik-kik-kik-kik calls of kingfishers
through the throaty harumph of old bull frogs,
through the shush-shush brush of dry limbs.
It's there she can forget her aching joints,
where she can lift gnarled fingers and touch
the wind, winding it like ribbons around her arm.
Wisdom blooms in the red-orange bromeliads,
and contentment sits on the backs of gators
stoically stretched beneath a burnished sun.

PART III | A MILLION LIVES

SKETCHING

I like the idea of you,
those lines I penciled in,
the shading of your eyes,
the curve of your cheeks,
just a bit too gaunt,
the subtle angled jaunt
of your adobe red beret;
I like the shading,
the slight blurring of charcoal
that gifted you
a devil-may-care grin;
I want to meet you,
to brush back the bangs
I swept across your forehead
and plant a kiss on the tip
of your Romanesque nose.

SUBWAY BLESSING

I study the gaunt face of the woman
who sits opposite me on the subway;
it's hard to tell her age—anywhere
between fifty and seventy I guess;
her dark skin is virtually unlined,
but there is something about her posture,
the slight slope of her back,
the weathered hands picking lint
from her plain black t-shirt
that tells me she's probably older.
She has a rucksack by her feet,
a newspaper and a plastic water bottle
sticking out the top;
I wonder if she's homeless,
if she rides the subway to keep warm.
Her coat has seen better years, as have
her dingy, once-white sneakers.
I have in mind to hand her a twenty,
but before I can leave my seat,
she stands and crosses over to mine.
I startle as she takes both my hands
in hers, thinking she might rob me.
But she just closes cocoa-brown eyes,
and in a gentle sing-song voice says,
"May the universe grant you peace;
may you find beauty and tranquility."

PART III | A MILLION LIVES

Faintly, in the background, I'm aware
of the conductor announcing the stop,
aware of the train pulling into the station.
The woman doesn't utter another word,
but simply stands, exits, fades into the crowd.
I close my gaping mouth and look at my palms,
goosebumps trailing up both arms. One thought
presses like a sacred kiss upon my forehead:
angels are never homeless.

THE TALISMAN

Head down, I mummer to myself, practicing answers for my interview. I can feel my palms growing damp, and I wipe them on my freshly-pressed black slacks. *Where do you see yourself in five years?* Man, I hate that one! I pull up short and stop just a breath away from a long orange feather with a just hint of white at the base. I start to step around it, but instead, bend down and pick it up. Ignoring my deceased mother's advice about mites, I stroke it against my fingers, luxuriating in its softness. It's a pigeon feather. Pigeons are a dime a dozen, as they say, in New York City, but this one, in the desert. This one! Probably one in a billion! I carefully put it in the front pocket of the binder I'd been clutching like a life raft and stride ahead, mapping out my next five years.

PART III | A MILLION LIVES

THOUGH WE DON'T SPEAK THE SAME LANGUAGE

we understand each other;
we understand the need for work,
for money to spend on the luxury
of putting bread in our mouths;
we understand we're not at the top
of the food chain,
but as our arms brush against each other
unloading the fishermen's catch of the day,
we grin conspiratorially,
both our faces weathered brown from the sun,
our hands raw and red from too much salt;
and we sing together, each in our own tongue,
our notes rivaling the screams of the seagulls,
neither of us caring if we're too loud or off-key;
we gesture with our hands; our bodies move as one,
slick with sticky sweat—we're the fastest team
on the docks, and we cling to that slice of fame;
at shift end, you fling your arm around my shoulder;
Gracious Dios, Thank God we were born
with kindred spirits and iron backs.

UNCONVENTIONAL EDUCATION

I called my dad adventurous;
others had different names for him:
irresponsible (from my mom),
good-for-nothing (from former bosses),
delinquent (from Principal Harris).
But when I was ten,
he was snow angels
on officially cancelled school days,
cross-country skiing
on days Dad cancelled himself,
steaming hot chocolate
in his double-wide trailer
where he would balance marshmallows
on the tip of his Roman nose.
He was shrieking laughter,
and pillow fights,
and eating bowls of mac & cheese
while watching MacGyver re-runs.
Everyone was always mad at him,
said he was the last person on earth
who should've had a kid,
but I thought he was the *only* person
on earth who should've had a kid.

PART III | A MILLION LIVES

UPON THIS I HITCHED MY DREAMS

too young and dumb
to know the difference
between love and lust,
a high-school sweetheart
was my ticket out of town;
riding shotgun
in a rusty pick-up truck,
we were going off to college,
he for business, me for nurse;
how naive at age eighteen
to hitch my dreams to a star
destined to explode
in the boundless universe;
turns out college girls
collect desires like keychains,
and straying eyes
often lead to straying hands;
what a fool to think
he was my forever;
dreams dispense into the ether
as soon as one awakes

Mosaic

WAITING FOR THE DIAGNOSIS

The day is sticky, like hot tar,
like super bubble bubblegum
on the bottom of a tennis shoe.
My four sisters and I clutch church fans,
the carboard kind with pictures of Jesus's face
stapled to a nice, long flat board stick,
the kind my grandma used to use
to fan away beads of sweat
when she got worked up about a sermon
or to give us swift rat-tap-taps on the head
if we started squirrelling around in the pew.
It's our mother's third trip to the doctor,
more specifically, the on-coly-gist,
which she says is just a fancy-pants word
for cancer doctor,
to make people feel more privileged
about having millions of rogue cells
mucking things up in their bodies.
The waiting room is stifling—
with heat, with anticipation,
with that space of time hovering
between   then   and   now
Mother emerges from behind closed doors,
the on-coly-gist on her heels.
She smiles, stiffly, I think,
and our fans pause in midair, each of our faces
turned like marionettes to hear the news.

PART III | *A MILLION LIVES*

"I don't have cancer," she says,
smiling more naturally now.
The room is silent for a moment,
the only sound a fly's futile attempts
to escape through a closed window—
then we erupt into whoops and shouts,
snot and tears streaming down our faces,
like we're in the middle of a tent revival,
and then we morph into one big lump
of flesh and sweat and salt.

THE WAY OF WATER POTS

stately heads,
necks of steel,
dusty feet calloused
by rocks and ruts;
an illusion of romance
when reality is steeped
in bearing the burden
of water carried
back to villages, to men,
to eager thirsty children;
dresses of orange, red, yellow
burn brightly on the horizon,
bangles jingle on sinewy arms
as each woman stares ahead,
her golden-brown eyes shadowing
the pain this three-mile walk will bear;
she will do it out of duty, out of love,
out of necessity because that's the way
it has always been done, by her mother,
by the mother before her and before her,
passing down wide hips and sturdy legs
and the expectation that a goddess born
enters the world with a pot upon her head.

PART III | A MILLION LIVES

WHEN YOU CALL ME MOMMA

The days turned into weeks;
weeks turned into months.
Surely there must be an aunt,
a sister, a cousin. . .
some maternal figure to lay
biological claim to a child
delivered to our door
at just two days old.
But no one came—except
exhausted social workers,
tangled up in red tape
and court dockets,
and the months
turned into years.
You don't understand time;
you don't realize
the difference in skin tone
or bloodlines.
You just press your nose
against mine,
touch your hand to my cheek
and say "Momma."
It's then I know everything
will be okay—in spite of my age,
when I should be empty nesting,
there is a reason I was chosen
to take you under my wings.

WHERE DREAMS ARE MADE

flashlights under chins,
we make ghoulish faces,
our shadows flickering
on wobbly canvas walls

there is just enough space
between house and woods
to create an independence
ten-year-old boys can enjoy

we stuff our round cheeks
with popcorn and cakes,
tell stories to make the hair
bristle stiffly on our arms,

dare each other to walk
ten paces from the tent,
double-dog dare for a hike
to the bank of Lost Creek

our skinny legs pumping,
we return from our dares,
hearts thumping with fear,
with adrenaline and dreams—

PART III | A MILLION LIVES

dreams of growing up,
of driving cars and working
as park rangers, of always
staying friends—just as we are

PART IV

A Million Natures

PART IV

PART IV | A MILLION NATURES

BENEATH THE SURFACE

I stare at the lake,
waves frothing
at its banks,
jewel-toned rocks
glistening
just below the surface,
the steady rhythm
laps against
the edges of my soul;
I'm a sister to the lake,
genetically inclined
to cast myself
upon the sand
to see whose toes
I touch,
hardwired to hide
my treasures
just deep enough
to make humans search
for the beautiful truth
of me, and even in
the grayest winter,
when my heart freezes
in mid stride,
there's an energy
underneath that says,
wait for me;
I'll be back in spring.

BONFIRE TRIOLET

Orange flames dance against the midnight sky;
music and laughter fill the space;
there's a quiet charm others long to find;
orange flames dance against the midnight sky.
None of us will ever wonder why
we keep returning to this place;
orange flames dance against the midnight sky;
music and laughter fill the space.

PART IV | A MILLION NATURES

CHAMOMILE AND POETRY

He's a simple man,
my uncle Jack—
can't read or write,
and it doesn't bother him.
We sit on his front porch
year round, (fall is my favorite)
he and I wrapped in quilts,
drinking our cups of chamomile
(Jack's favorite bedtime tea).
He says, Emma, look there—
see all those *words*?
Some are robin-belly red,
dangling from the trees,
some are puffing up
that old bullfrog's throat,
others are the paintbrush
that set the sky ablaze,
and those, way up there,
Emma. . .those are covering
the mountain peaks
with heaps of powder snow.
I follow his gnarled fingers,
and think, poets don't need
to write; they only need
to adore the world.

CONFESSIONAL

leaves bowed
beneath the wind,
I take my cue,
bow my head, too
dark clouds my chapel,
thunder my priest,
forgiven by rain,
sins released

PART IV | *A MILLION NATURES*

HOPE COMES IN YELLOW

Skiffs of snow,
an everlasting winter,
tree branches bleak,
stiff with melancholy,
but there, in the yard,
cold-defying
stalks of green
tipped with buds
of yellow,
miniature balls of sun,
the promise of spring

THE LOVELY ALONE

the stars are alive tonight,
winking silvery pinpricks
piercing a black velvet sky;
I feel at once both small
and majestic,
robed as I am in a downy quilt
and slippered feet;
I was made for this—
this slice of solitude
filled only with the trill of tree frogs
and cricket violins;
a red bonfire glows
warmly against my face;
I nestle into my Adirondack chair
and wrap my fingers around
a steaming mug of honeyed tea;
this is it—
all I want,
all I need,
the quintessence of peace

PART IV | *A MILLION NATURES*

MY TRIP TO THE MOON TRIOLET

I blew bubbles on the moon,
free of gravity.
Space birds sang a gorgeous tune;
I blew bubbles on the moon.
The time to leave came too soon,
but I will not forget;
I blew bubbles on the moon,
free of gravity.

RECOVERY

dusty brown soil
leached of nutrients
lies beneath
an unrelenting sun,
a helpless skinned pelt
scarred with fissures,
unable to sustain
a single blade of grass;
three months gone
without a hint of moisture,
distant thunder rumbles,
marbles in a tin cup—
nothing but a promise
unfulfilled;
then one weary evening
in blows a west wind
gathering up the grays,
a fat nimbostratus
pregnant with hope;
      the first plump drops
bring the children running,
bring the grownups praying,
each inhaling
tangy petrichor,
little tongues extended,
hands wet with hallelujahs,
earth's acceptance,
a baptism overdue.

PART IV | *A MILLION NATURES*

ROOM TO BREATHE

I broke free of skyscrapers,
      free of concrete,
      free of freeways,
      free of suits,
office-gray cubicles,
long lines at the coffee shop,
overpriced bagels and lattes;
some called it a mid-life crisis;
I called it coming to my senses,
although I have to admit
the new yellow convertible
smacked of middle-40s.
But I never felt more authentically
me—the first time I saw a sunset
      free of obstructions,
      free of constraints,
      free to blaze like flames
in the wide Nebraska sky.

Mosaic

A SERENGETI CORN FIELD

A lone tree stands in a field,
backlit by a tangerine sun,
a hint of fog skirting its trunk
like a dancer's gauzy tutu.
It appears strange and exotic
as though I've been transported
to the untamed Serengeti.
I envision a herd of giraffes striding past,
their long, graceful necks extended
as they graze on tender leaves.
And I'm suddenly overcome with gratitude,
for the sun that has warmed its branches,
for the rains that have nourished its roots,
for the generations of flannel-clad farmers
who have plowed around its trunk
year after year to plant their beans and corn.
Someone, long ago, thought this single tree
worth saving, and thus it has remained—
an indigenous remnant of nature
on the edge of Mid-West suburbia.

PART IV | *A MILLION NATURES*

SHEDDING

Come, sweet spring, push brown earth
held fast in winter's teeth.
Raise timid moss-green stems;
say prayers with daffodils.
Serve up tangy blossoms,
tissue-thin with tempered hope
of yielding summer's fruit.
Ride on the robin's breast,
a song upon your lips.
The dead have had their due;
It's time to live again.
My curls bounce in the breeze;
I shed my somber coat.

STEPPING BACK

Just for a moment,
on one of the warmest days
of the new spring,
I stopped being a grownup and
walked barefoot through the grass,
picked a dandelion,
rubbed it under my chin
to see if I was in love,
climbed onto a low tree branch
and listened to the bees humming
in the pink crabapple blossoms,
closed my eyes and saw myself,
at age ten, swinging my legs
over branches much higher up,
reading mystery books,
sipping sweet tea.
I hop down and lie on the ground,
soaking in the tender rays of sun
and warm-soil memories.

PART IV | *A MILLION NATURES*

TENDER YEAR

a slender branch is
bendable in its greenness,
too new to be broken,
saturated with dappled
spring sun, a supple
recipient of raindrops—

it's in this hallowed space
of time the branch grows
among the knotted wise
but still resists the hand
of nature urging it to bear
a thicker skin

TIME OUT

I remove myself
from shoulders and elbows
jostling for position,
the stiff staccato beat
of a million harried feet.
I trade traffic lights
for skies pinpricked with stars,
high-rises for pines,
the smell of exhaust and sweat
for the dewy dampness of soil.
I curl cat-like on my blanket,
content to spoon the moon,
and fall asleep to the serenade
of crickets on the bluff.

THESE BRAVE BRANCHES

though they tremble
in the wind
though they bear the weight
of leaves and feet
though they bend at the waist
under storms' heavy hands
though they are stripped bare
by cold November rains
though they are held prisoner
       in winter's cruel talons
they shall remain
       resolute, resourceful,
waiting for the life blood
       of spring

WASTING DAYS TRIOLET

I languish under a paper sun
suppressed by winter's hand,
tired before the day's begun;
I languish under a paper sun.
My blue mind has come undone;
I need summer's breath.
I languish under a paper sun
suppressed by winter's hand.

PART IV | A MILLION NATURES

WINTER SOLSTICE

The days grow shorter;
night squeezes the life
out of dinner time,
brings out the yawns
by 7 p.m.
Standing in pajamas,
I touch the cold glass,
my reflection
staring back at me—
a slightly haggard
version of myself.
Today is the day,
I whisper—*Solstice,
Solstitium:
the sun stands still.*
I hold my breath;
the earth holds its breath;
there's an imperceptible
      shift
a creaking of joints,
a creaking of an axis.
The days grow longer;
the spool of light unwinds:
three more minutes,
five more minutes,
ten more minutes
      until—

MOSAIC

the sun touches my dinner plate,
my fork, my hand, my face.
I blink but don't close the blinds.
This is it, I think. *I'm going to survive
another winter.*

PART IV | *A MILLION NATURES*

WINTER WEIGHT

I grow thin
in the winter,
eating slices of sun
no bigger than the edge
of a tea cup;

the wind howls
in the winter,
forcing me to wrap
my feet, my hands
my naked face;

squirrels grow fat
in the winter,
eating leftover seeds
I give to birds
that flew North;

I grow weary
in the winter,
my brain heavy
with unreleased
serotonin,
pressed by clouds;

Mosaic

squirrels grow fat
in the winter,
mocking me
with cheerful tails,
cheeks full
of freedom.

PART V

A Million Giggles

PART V | A MILLION GIGGLES

35TH CLASS REUNION

They gather us up from
the four corners of the earth,
like folding crumbs into
a dinner napkin.

We mingle, awkwardly,
among fairy lights
and half-faded memories
of whom was dating whom
back in the day.

Brains go into overdrive
trying to put a name to that face!
A face we undoubtedly sat beside
in freshman algebra.

Daniel? David? Devon—something?
Wait—did he even go to our school?

Drinks flow and people begin to relax;
soon there is raucous laughter,
and the by-gone cliques
begin to clump together
like sticky little rice balls. . .
they can't help themselves.

Mosaic

Some have fared better than others—
probably using moisturizer or Botox;
definitely making frequent trips to the salon;
girl, that shade of blonde comes from a box!
A few of the guys have lost their hair
but are still miles ahead of two crack heads
who have lost their teeth.

(Weren't they voted least likely to succeed?)

We talk marriages and divorces
(a record holder has six of each)
We talk kids, colleges, and careers;
Someone starts singing karaoke,
and a few beers later
we fling our arms around each other,
swaying gently to "Open Arms" by Journey,

and swear that our high school years
were the *best times* of our lives;

we get all weepy,
and blow snot into cute
travel tissues that someone
(Maggie? Mira?) pulls from
her purse, and we part with
"We should do this more often."

But we won't. See you at our 40.

PART V | A MILLION GIGGLES

ALL IN THE FAMILY

the uncle with roving hands,
the aunt who's been married
      to the twin uncles
(different times, naturally)
the cousin known for tall tales
and a short temper,
the brother who carries a gun
when he uses the john,
his motto: never get caught
with your pants down,
the sister
and half sister
and step sister
and half-step sister—
their favorite mixed drink:
Sex on the Beach,
the uncle who chain-smokes,
his mother who chain-crochets,
the grandpa and ex-grandpa
who come to blows over horseshoes,
but never over the grandma
who left them both and moved to Vegas;
it's a zoo, a shit-show,
a shiver down the spine—
my blood is theirs;
their blood is mine.

MOSAIC

THE BEST EXES

the kind who will not
pop up on the street,
in the store,
during church service
(and make you lose
your religion),
the kind who is resolved
to change—
somewhere else
on someone else's dime,
to check out self-help books
from a library five states over,
five countries over,
(never hurts to adopt
a foreign language),
the kind who can read
the subtitles on your face
and just know, by sheer
unnatural instinct
that some things
are better left unsaid,
the kind who will not
let you down
by turning up
on your doorstep
dripping with the notion
that you will take him back.

PART V | *A MILLION GIGGLES*

A BOY'S POCKETS

In doing all the laundry
boys' pants are just the worst,
all the things I find in pockets
make me want to curse,
sometimes I find paperclips
and bits of broken rocks
other times it's chocolate bars
and even dirty socks,
but the worst surprise I ever had
(besides a fur ball from the dog)
was a squishy wriggling thing—
a living, breathing frog!

BUFFERING

Exhaustion sits
on my slumped shoulders,
in the curve of my spine;
it travels down my calves
and settles into the arches
of my feet;
I'm a video—frozen,
unable to respond.
I just need a pause,
a chance to buffer,
a chance to spin
in that blissful, circular
space—
close my eyes,
yoga breathe,
doze off in the recliner.
I promise
the video can resume.
I will reconnect;
I just need time.

PART V | A MILLION GIGGLES

CAN I GET A REFUND?

eyes blurry from lack of sleep,
a toddler up at o'dark thirty,
snot and tears and tug-of-war
over a pair of shoes,
a pop tart to eat in the car,
(shall we call that breakfast)?
a million little fires
to put out before collection;
with each turn, I see a flame;
I'm too old for this,
too young for this.
I grab the adult-life receipt,
a purchase made years ago
in a moment of haste and a fit
      of inspiration.
Can I get a refund—
a *full* refund that allows
for sleep
for eating a meal in peace
for reading an entire book
(also in peace)
for the ability to hop into a car
without buckles, belts, wailing,
bags ladened with snacks and wipes
for shopping without a list?
I see it now—*no refunds allowed*;
I should've read the fine print.

A CARD-CARRYING MEMBER OF THE PASSIVE AGGRESSIVE CLUB

I love it when you say
Fine, whatever!
Love it when your barbed remarks
stay just below the fence line,
and that little twitchy thing
you do with your mouth,
that slight raise of one eyebrow,
is classic artistry.
I live for the cloak and dagger
disapproval,
little digs that speak volumes
beneath your muted breath.
I truly cannot thank you enough
for your sabotage and subterfuge.
Hang onto your card, honey;
it's going platinum!

PART V | A MILLION GIGGLES

COMFORT FOOD

hot melted cheese
bubbling in pasta
eyes closed,
mouth parted,
sorrow soon forgotten
buried
in that first delectable
taste on the tongue

pint-size carton
fresh from the freezer,
creamy chocolate,
swirls of caramel,
tears melt away
as the spoon sinks
into icy bliss

yeasty smell
of golden bread
fresh from the oven,
yellow butter
on each slice,
gray clouds part
sunshine on fingers

MOSAIC

COUNTING GEESE

Please excuse my poor excuses
for counting geese (or is it gooses)
while lying down upon the hill
instead of traveling to the mill;
I know the grain won't grind itself,
and we'll have no bread upon the shelf,
but I just had to stop and ponder,
do geese wonder when they wander?

PART V | *A MILLION GIGGLES*

DOES WANTING COUNT?

I clip coupons I'll never use
because I *want* to use them;
I imagine myself shopping wisely,
pulling out each little coupon
at the checkout counter
as if I am a highly organized
penny-conscious human being.
I look up easy exercise programs
because I want to exercise;
well, no—I don't *really* want to,
but I know I need to,
so, I imagine myself on a yoga mat,
dutifully stretching, kicking my legs,
counting reps in my head,
dabbing a bit of sweat from my brow
when it's thankfully over.
I write down exotic recipes
because I want to be a talented chef
because I can imagine buying things
like Ceylon cinnamon bark, organic
ginger, and kimchi flavored sea salt.
When I have company, I want to say,
Oh, this old dish? Why it's just a little
thing called Indian Lamb Beryani.

Mosaic

ENLIGHTEN ME

oh, great one
full of knowledge,
I am waiting—
a blank slate
designed to absorb
your every thought;
impart your wisdom,
use big vocabulary;
I love it when you talk
      Dictionary;
I'll spend nights
dissecting the meaning;
you, oh, cosmic one,
on your seat next to God,
how have I survived this long
without you pointing out
my every imperfection?
I'll kiss the ground you walk on,
now that I have seen your holy shoes;
where would I be
if not under your feet?

PART V | A MILLION GIGGLES

THE FACE OF A THOUSAND WORDS

I keep words inside my throat
that are not polite to say;
although this man is arrogant,
he cannot ruin my day.

I listen to his endless chatter,
the focus all on him;
any chance I might escape
is looking pretty slim.

He's been around the world it seems
and owns a hundred cars;
a tiger once attacked him,
and—oh, look, there's the scar!

He's showing me his biceps now,
and, oops—there goes my grace
every word I'd left unsaid
is now written on my face!

MOSAIC

GET A CAT THEY SAID

it will be fun they said,
except I'm only allowed to pet him
every other Thursday,
and now I need a new couch.

I'M OLD ENOUGH

to discuss hemorrhoids
and the subsequent
treatments thereof;
I'm old enough to select
the most effective denture cream
and joke with the 60-year-old cashier
that she's young enough to be my daughter;
I'm old enough to pre-plan how to get up
if I take a tumble (providing nothing is broken),
and I'm old enough to babble about
the *good old days*
even though I've seen the teeth of war;
I'm old enough to wake up so I don't pee the bed
and old enough to find dignity in adult pullups;
I'm old enough to check my blood pressure
twice a day and keep my doctor appointments;
I'm old enough to carry around just enough sass
as is expected (and respectable) in an old man,
but I'm too young to have my name in the obituaries,
and until they make a coffin that looks like
a fishing boat, I ain't setting one foot in the ground.

THE INTROVERTED EXTROVERT

Pardon me if I say no;
I can't go to the movies,
can't host a party,
can't purchase your candles
or your cookware;
I'd rather eat at home.
My people meter
has expired,
and I have no spare change.
So I'll regroup,
rest both mind and spirit,
and someday I'll say yes.
Someday
I'll put a little extro on my intro
and rejoin the human race.

I USED TO

vacuum, notice fingerprints
        on windows,
plump pillows, sweep floors,
        remove dust,
wash sheets every week,
        plan ahead,
read a book in blissful silence,
        drink hot tea,
but children rearranged life,
        got up early,
didn't sleep through the night,
        fingerprinted
every surface in the house,
        pooped on carpet,
pulled books from their shelves,
        spilled lemonade,
raised such a noxious ruckus,
        no one could think,
let alone read a book in peace,
        and so it goes,
my ducks used to be in a row,
        but they escaped;
perhaps I will find them one day
        beneath the jellied couch.

MOSAIC

JUST SOUTH OF SANITY

Gwen's off her meds,
my mom would say,
and quirk her mouth up
in a half grin;
her sister was a little nuts,
if we were all being politically incorrect,
but not in the hide-your-knives-when-she-comes-over
kind of way,
just in that quirky-batty way,
the way she'd scrape icing off a slice of cake,
cut the cake into little pieces
then dip each piece in the scraped off icing,
the way she'd tell us all to hold hands
at the dinner table then sing the chorus
of *Shall We Gather at the River* as the blessing,
the way she'd rub a raggedy old rabbit's foot
that dangled from the end of a keychain for good luck;
honestly though, Aunt Gwen was (to us kids anyway)
        jalapeno peppers on ice cream.
She was glitter and fingerpaints on the walls (sorry Mom);
she was stomping in mud puddles until you were soaked through;
she was carrying a Chihuahua in her purse to Sunday service;
we just giggled behind our unlined hands and secretly hoped
she'd never pop another pill as long as she lived.

PART V | A MILLION GIGGLES

THE LONGEST RIDE

canned music tinkles
through the speakers,
shoulder-to-shoulder,
faces intently study
the lighted numbers
10, 9, 8—ding,
two passengers
unknot themselves
from the pack
and disembark,
shuffling, a cough,
someone hits
the close door button
then everyone resumes
ardent concentration
as if the numbers
can coat the silence
the way honey
coats the throat,
7, 6, 5—ding
the door opens,
four people enter
one couple says,
we'll wait for the next one
4—stop
3—stop
ground floor, finally;

Mosaic

    the door slides open
    people disperse,
    fluttering and chattering
    like birds
    after the storm has passed

THE LUCKIEST GIRL TRIOLET

Friday the thirteenth is her lucky day;
she pets every black cat;
she sees a ladder and saunters that way;
Friday the thirteenth is her lucky day.
She never throws spilled salt away,
especially not over her back.
Friday the thirteenth is her lucky day;
she pets every black cat.

MOSAIC

MIDNIGHT MAZE

Did I lock the door? When Susan said *nice slacks*—did she mean pretty, shapely, high-class slacks? Should I fix baked ziti or chicken fettuccine for Friday dinner? When was the last time I shaved my legs? They feel a little prickly. Can I wear white after Memorial Day? When is Memorial Day? May something. I should probably plant flowers soon. And put out hummingbird feeders. What flowers do hummingbirds like? How small is a baby hummingbird? My friend, Jenny is having a baby. I should make some booties. Do people still make booties? Wait—did Susan think my booty looked too big in my slacks?

bumping into walls
cheese
always out of reach

PART V | *A MILLION GIGGLES*

MY CONVERSATION WITH AN EARTHWORM

As I was digging through the soil
to plant my beans in rows,
I almost chopped an earthworm
with my garden hoe.
I apologized immediately
and took him from the bed,
but when I turned him end to end
I forgot which was his head.
"Excuse me sir," I said to him,
"I can't tell head from tail."
It would have been much easier
if I'd been talking to a snail.

OH, EMILY

up in your room
wearing white,
pacing the floor
with pen and paper,
curling letters
out of iron bars,
rhymes slanted
like April rain,
tucking death
beneath
the floorboards,
I'm sorry, Em;
I don't get it—
all that beauty
brought to bloom
posthumously!
(thanks to your
treacherous sister).
Not me, love!
I'm flinging ink
(the confetti of my soul)
for all the world to see
long before *Death*
'kindly stops for me.'

*A tribute to Emily Dickinson

PART V | *A MILLION GIGGLES*

PERHAPS GOD IS WAITING FOR A HALLELUJAH

prim, proper—nearly stoic,
people lined into orderly pews,
dresses, stockings, ties, and suits,
voices keeping a low-key rhythm
with mouths opening and shutting
like good little fish,
the sacraments are in tidy plastic cups,
the offering baskets dutifully passed,
the three-point sermon tied with ribbon,
but
what if God is holding his breath—
what if he's waiting for a little stirring,
a little swaying of the hips,
hands waving to heaven,
heads thrown back in abandoned;
what if he's waiting for a glory-hallelujah,
waiting for feet to dance like David did
before the Lord,
and what if God came down and stormed
the pulpit with a hell, fire, and brimstone
sermon that shook the rafters, raised the roof,
and what if he said, *Can I get an Amen?*

PLEASE EXCUSE MY OCD

So, I'm a little bit peculiar;
I like my desk so-so,
I keep my pencils all lined up
in pretty little rows;
the stapler's always to my right,
beside my paper tray;
there's a holder for each folder,
the tabs on full display.
Lesson plans are color coded,
each in their own file;
I suggest you *do not touch*
if you want to see me smile!

PART V | A MILLION GIGGLES

THE RECIPE OF MY TRIBE

½ cup of OCD
2 heaping cups of sass
1 full stick of hug-it-out
a pinch of real kick-ass
¾ cup of therapy
1 cup of half-past-youth
5 tablespoons of loyalty
3 cups of brutal truth.

MOSAIC

RUNNING LATE

My timing is so terrible,
as in I'm always late;
where do all those minutes go;
I don't even know the date!
I really try to watch the clock
but the hands just run away,
and before I even count to ten
there goes the whole darn day.
I'm late to weddings, late to brunch
late to yoga too!
I need a family intervention;
I don't know what else to do.
They all say I need to focus
and organize my time,
but if I'm always late to funerals,
I'm sure I'll be late to mine.

PART V | A MILLION GIGGLES

A SINGLE CROW

Just my luck
(or not)
to see a single crow
perched on the roof
of the high-rise apartment complex.
I probably wouldn't have noticed
except for his persistent
cawwww. . .cawwww,
his raising of such a ruckus
that my head jerked up
as though it was on a string,
and (as I am one to avoid
spilling salt
and walking under ladders)
I shuddered a bit
to see that solitary oil-colored
fiend and felt a full-chill flashback—
(a certain high school English raven)!
Had there been two crows,
I would have been safe,
but, in the spirit of bad omens,
I narrowly escaped
the deadly trajectory
of a potted fern
flung from balcony #405.

TOO PEOPLEY OUT THERE

I know I'm not the only one
who sits in the dark
on my bathroom floor
and has a good cry
because the bumps and bruises
of too many bodies
got the better of me
because honking horns
and flipped middle birds
sent me into flight mode,
away from the talons
of traffic—
back to my burrow
with its cool tile floors,
where I collect breaths,
rewire the circuit board,
and prep to rejoin
the mass population.

PART VI

A Million Triumphs

PART 1

PART VI | *A MILLION TRIUMPHS*

BEAUTIFUL BARBED WIRE

Unwind the roll,
silver in the sun;
it glints with promises
of boundaries.

BUILDING BRIDGES

hand me a plank;
I'll hand you a saw;
together we will build
a bridge across this chasm;
we'll all be brothers and sisters,
sweating together beneath a sun
hung in the universe for all mankind,
drinking water from our father's wells;
we will remove the shards of hate
and bind up every wound,
acknowledging all blood is red
and thus in need of healing.

CRY ME A RIVER

You always did have a flair
for drama, didn't you?
Never one to waste a crisis.
Never one to pass up
an opportunity to stir the pot,
to poke the hornet's nest.
Funny how you always managed
to look so surprised
when someone retaliated,
baring claws and teeth,
as if you had no idea
the damage you'd caused.
Hollywood actors have won Oscars
for less theatrics.
But it's all out, now—isn't it?
The jig is up, as they say;
everyone's got your number.
So, stir and poke away;
no one will come running
to see about all the fuss;
no one will ask if you're OK.
Everyone has managed
to move on without you,
to heal and grow and thrive—
and there's not one soul left
to wipe your tears.

DID I

well, pardon me
did I hurt your egg-shell ego

did I tear down the façade
you worked so hard to build

did I not cover up the bruise
with enough foundation

did I expose a secret
you never wished to tell

did I fall short of expectations
to be seen but never heard

did I clean out the closet
with too much cloak and dagger

did I slip through your fingers
like sand gone through a sieve

PART VI | *A MILLION TRIUMPHS*

EXPECTATIONS

It is expected, ma'am,
that you have dinner ready,
put on petal-pink lipstick...

It is expected, sir,
that I will cook when I'm ready,
just depends on my schedule,

It is expected, sweetie,
that you watch your tongue,
be seen and not heard...

It is expected, *honey*,
that I will speak
whenever I damn well please,

It is expected, darling,
that you leave politics to the men,
no need for hysterics...

It is expected, dear,
that I will vote and march
in solidarity and sisterhood

it's time to bend
the arc of boundaries

GHOSTED

the way I slipped out,
a wisp in the dark—
it's as though
I never existed;
and this new anonymity—
it's my drink of choice!
You cannot grasp a ghost.

THE GREAT AWAKENING

He saw me in the garden,
tracked my methodical
wanderings
across green leaves;
he pitied me, I suppose,
in my ungainly state
of plump satisfaction.
Let me help you, he said,
and he smothered me
with jewels and chiffon—
around and around,
wound and wound,
until I stopped resisting,
until I sat in the dark,
until I fell asleep.
When I awoke,
when I yawned and stretched,
when I broke through the confines
that had held me bound so long,
I shivered with unexpected energy.
He was still there, of course,
awaiting my transformation,
a thing for which he could take
full credit—
but I looked at the arch of trees,
stretched my feathery new wings
to their full, glorious breadth
and flew beyond his oversight.

THE HOUSES I BUILT

Young and naïve,
what did I know of red flags?
I said I do and built a house of straw.
It was warm enough, safe enough—
until you blew it down.
I stared at the straw around my feet,
stunned but determined to try harder.
Next, I built a house of sticks—
spoke in shorter sentences,
learned to walk on egg shells;
you wrecked that house too.
The sticks left bruises no one wanted
to talk about–I'd made my bed.
Shouldn't I have to lie in it?
But I stood again, straighter this time,
my feet planted shoulder-width apart.
I grabbed mortar and bricks,
stacked them one row at a time,
a citadel in the making.
Oh, how red your face became when you
                huffed and puffed;
I thought your cheeks would explode!
But you couldn't budge the bricks,
not even an inch.
You're welcome to try the chimney,
but I've made a fire as hot as hell.

PART VI | *A MILLION TRIUMPHS*

THE HUMMINGBIRDS WILL RETURN

I stare wistfully at empty feeders,
but the tiny birds who have darted
about all summer have flown south,
drawn to warmer climates—
they seem to know, before we do,
that imminent change is coming,
the trading of t-shirts for sweaters
and shorts for joggers or jeans,
but I know they will return
after the leaves have fallen,
after the wind has swept them away,
after snow has covered the ground,
after daffodils bring a yellowed spring;
we need only to wait out the seasons
and to believe in the power of change.

MOSAIC

I'M ALONE BUT NOT LONELY

a table for one means reading
and sipping raspberry iced tea;
I can stretch in my sea of a bed,
dog by my side comically growling
in the throes of a squirrelly dream;
I can eat chocolate for breakfast,
or oatmeal—or skip it altogether;
birds chirp outside my window
as if they have the whole planet
to themselves;
I'm alone but not lonely;
the sound of cultured voices,
the smells of a dozen cuisines
waft across the apartment courtyard,
and at any given moment
I might be in India sitting down to curry
or sailing down the French Riviera
sipping a glass of Bordeaux;
I'm alone but not lonely;
I chat to friends and neighbors
then leave them,
each to their own porches,
balconies, and chic Zen gardens;
I dance to the beat of my own drum,
hips swaying with the wind,
bare toes tapping in tandem;
I'm alone but not lonely

PART VI | A MILLION TRIUMPHS

INVINCIBLE SUMMER

always there
just beneath the surface;
axis tipped closer to the sun,
I return
from the winter battle
riding a white horse—
blazing sword in hand,
freedom dripping
from unfrozen lips

LINE IN THE SAND

I've learned to recognize the signs:
the crossed arms, the swaying
from side to side;
it's the manic in her,
water spilling through the cracks,
the dam-about-to-break.
I've learned less is more;
some people must be loved
from a distance.
There's no cure for what ails her,
although a well-trained
psychiatrist might disagree,
heralding the virtues
of therapy and meds.
But he doesn't know her like I do—
doesn't know
about the self-medication
or the amber liquid
used to swallow pills.
He doesn't know
that she has a master's in manipulation,
or that the long shadows of her narcissism
cast blame on everyone but herself.
We're good, though—
                she on her side,
me on mine.

PART VI | A MILLION TRIUMPHS

NOT THE END OF MY STORY

the book spine creaks
as though it will break,
cold   stiff,
unyielding;
frozen in the past,
      it trembles with the weight,
the absolute solemnity,
of opening   of moving forward;
it's been painfully comfortable here,
on this bed of thorns,
my blood scattered
      in tiny droplets
across indelible ink,
but I can't stay   here;
I know that now;
and so, I rise,
my legs tingling
from prolonged disuse;
fresh pen in hand,
I take stock of my scars,
      the people, the places
that put them there,
and I begin to write
a new chapter.

MOSAIC

THERE'S SOMETHING ABOUT THE REARVIEW

No regrets,
the house is getting smaller,
a white dot in the rearview,
now disappearing 'round the bend;
full tank of gas, foot on the pedal,
suitcase in the back seat;
there's freedom in the wind.
Love how the dirt road
changes into blacktop,
the cow-dotted landscape
becomes an honest town.
No one believed me
when I said I'd go to college,
but they're in the rearview;
Look at me now!

PART VI | A MILLION TRIUMPHS

THE UNDERDOG

a long shot,
that's what they say
when you're lying dormant
beneath layers of ice,
when no one has seen you
in the thousand-day winter;
even the birds can't scritch
and scratch enough
to get to the heart of you;
truth is, you haven't been still—
you've been conserving energy,
quietly growing,
pushing upward
a little each day;
you smile—imaging the faces
of those who counted you out,
those who said you'd never make it,
those who dismissed you
with a cursory nod;
you can feel the vibrations of earth,
subtle warmth seeping into the soil;
you are ready—
this is your moment;
you take a deep breath
and heave—

Mosaic

    breaking barriers
    breaking winter's back
    and emerge,
    arms outstretched,
    elated face upturned
    toward a vibrant sun.

PART VI | A MILLION TRIUMPHS

WHAT A BEAUTIFUL MESS

you made with the slamming door,
breaking the mosaic of you and me,
scattering pieces across the floor,

but I picked up just enough shards
of blues and greens and tangerines
to create a stunning masterpiece

who answers to no one

MOSAIC

WOMAN FROM THE RIB

skin as soft as rose petals,
a body moldable, bendable,
the ability to wrap around children,
protect them from the inside out,
all the vulnerability
to make her
        breakable,
a heart of fine china
instead of Melamine;
but couldn't her bones have been made
a little bit stronger,
especially the ulna and the radius?
        perhaps God could've invested
in ground-breaking bionics
designed to ward off blows
launched at the face or skull;
I mean, think of it,
a bionic-armed woman!
        but then where would it have ended—
steel spine
reinforced ribs
supersonic legs?
How would she have known her place?
So, she got bones, just plain old bones
(protein, collagen, calcium)
shaped from the rib of a man,

PART VI | A MILLION TRIUMPHS

and it would take pages and pages
of history, bound together
with the most resolute glue,
generation after generation
        to sharpen her brain
        to give her a voice
        to create her own steel
so that she, woman born of rib,
could stand on her own clay feet.

A WORK IN PROGRESS

break out the orange barrels,
the orange cones,
the flashing signs:
speed limit 45 mph;
get the excavators,
bulldozers,
pavers—
I'm going to need them all;
can't really give a completion date,
this stretch of me
contains a juggernaut
of potholes,
erosion from too many cars
riding on my back;
I'm a bit broken, you see,
a little unsafe,
but once I'm paved,
you'll barely see
the scars.

PART VI | A MILLION TRIUMPHS

YOU WILL LOOK

but you won't find me;
I've erased that girl
with a pink block eraser,
wiped out the fear,
the insecurities,
the timidity;
no! when you look,
you'll pass me by;
I'm unrecognizable
with my chin up,
my head held high;
there's finesse in my steps,
fire in my eyes;
were you to glance my way,
you'd think I was someone else,
and I am;
I've shucked off the layers
of people pleasing
and stand transformed
in my own brave skin.

Acknowledgments

Amethyst (online July 23, 2024)
"There's a Meadow"

Anacapa Review (*Gunpowder Press*) (Vol. 2 Issue 1 Jan. 2024)
"Sketching"
"Fade to Black"

(The) Banyan Review (Issue 19 Fall 2024)
"Aging Out"

Boats Against the Current (online Feb. 27, 2024)
"Everyone Smiles but the Clown"

Cholla Needles (issue 87 Feb. 2024)
"Final Symphony"
"Wasting Days Triolet"
"The Talisman"
"The Hands that Held"
"Beautiful Barbed Wire"
"Clementine Stockings"
"Worn around the Edges"

(Issue 92 July 2024)
"Invincible Summer"
"My Skin Feels Slick with Grief"
"My Trip to the Moon"

A C K N O W L E D G M E N T S

"Shedding"
"The Cabin Cat"
"Some Things Won't Bear the Weight of Words
"Confessional"

The Coalition (Issue 8 July 2024)
"The Longest Ride"
"Cold Shoulder"
"No Words"

Contemporary Haibun Online (Aug. 2024 Issue 20.2)
"Midnight Maze"

The Dewdrop (online May 5, 2024)
"A Serengeti Cornfield"

Door is A Jar (Issue 32 Fall 2024)
"The Houses I Built"

Five Fleas Itchy Poetry (online March 22, 2024)
"Get a Cat They Said"
"The Recipe of My Tribe"

Freshwater Literary Review (online May 2024)
"Recall of a Soldier"
"Winter Solstice"

Fresh Words Magazine (Feb. 2024 online issue)
"Dear Daughter"

GAS: Poetry, Art & Music (online Dec. 28, 2023—Featured Poet)
"Time Out"
"Oh, Child of Mine"
"The Breath"

(online June 27, 2024)
"Neurodivergent Processing"

Acknowledgments

"Room to Breathe"
"You Know"
"Meet Me By the River"
"Runner"

Green Silk Journal (online Oct. 30, 2024)
"A Division of Goods"

Halcyon Times (Premier Issue 1 June 2024)
"Chamomile and Poetry"
"Stepping Back"

Havik (May 2024 Issue)
"Woman from a Rib"
"The Best Exes" *won feature piece honorable mention
"All in the Family"

Homer's Odyssey Magazine (online June 28, 2024)
"Unconventional Education"
"Too Young to Know"

The Hooghly Review (online July 21, 2024)
"Just South of Sanity"
"A Card-Carrying Member of the Passive Aggressive Club"
"The Luckiest Girl Triolet"
"A Single Crow"
"The Face of a Thousand Words"

Humana Obscura (March Spring 2024 Issue)
"Hope Comes in Yellow"

The Lake (March 2024 Issue)
"Oh, Emily"

Last Leaves Literary Magazine
"A Trap of Your Own Making" (Issue 9 Oct. 2024)
"Too Peopley Out There" (Issue 8 April 2024)
"The Keeping Room" (Issue 8 April 2024)

Acknowledgments

Last Stanza Poetry (Issue 17 July 2024)
"The Spanish Moss Chronicles"

Literary Heist
"Cry Me a River" (online Feb. 2024)
"The Urns We Carry" (online June 2024)

Literary Yard (online July 28, 2024)
"Building Bridges"
"Baker's Cabinet"
"The Introverted Extrovert"
"The Fall of Us"
"Mama and Papa's Dance" (online Oct. 13, 2024)
"Once Around the Block" (online Oct. 13, 2024)

Lothlorien Poetry Journal (online April 26, 2024)
"Perhaps God is Waiting for a Hallelujah"
"Enlighten Me"
"Phantom Pain"

MacQueen Quinterly
"The Way Back" (Issue 25 Sept.)*long-listed finalist
"Unmended" (Issue 24 August) *short-listed finalist

Modern Literature
"Reversal of Roles" (online Feb. 4, 2024)
"Patterns" (online Feb. 4, 2024)
"Can I Get a Refund?" (online March 5, 2024)
"Subway Blessing" (forthcoming Dec. 2024)
"Too Young to Know" (online March 5, 2024)
"We Used to" (online March 5, 2024)

The Monterey Poetry Review (Fall 2024 Issue)
"The Apple Peeler"
"When My Metabolism was Young"
"Comfort Food"

ACKNOWLEDGMENTS

Naugatuck River Review (Winter/Spring 2024 issue)
"Light from Within"

Northwest Indiana Literary Journal (online Sept. 18, 2024)
"Expectations"

October Hill Magazine
"Passed Down" (Vol. 7 Issue 4 Winter 2023)
"Winter Weight" (Vol. 7 Issue 4 Winter 2023)
"You Will Look" (Vol. 8 Issue 2 Summer 2024)
"I'm Alone but Not Lonely" (Vol. 8 Issue 2 Summer 2024)

Of Rust and Glass (Issue 17 July 2024 "Sacrifices")
"As The Candle Burns"

One Art Poetry (online Aug. 25, 2024)
"The Only Photo"

Orange Juice (Issue 1 July 2024)
"When You Call Me Momma"

Paddler Press (*Firelight and Footprints: Poetry from the Canoe and Campsite 2024*)
"My Conversation with a Heron"
"Bonfire Triolet"
"Where Dreams are Made"

Poetry Breakfast (online July 17, 2024)
"A Work in Progress"

Poet's Espresso Review (Vol. 14 Issue 6 Fall 2024)
"The Sun Always Rises"
"Beneath the Surface"

Prosetrics: The Literary Magazine (Issue 8 Sept. 2024)
"The Hummingbirds Will Return"

Acknowledgments

Rat's Ass Review
"Butterfly" (Spring-Summer 2024 Issue)
"The Last Drive In Movie Theater" (forthcoming Fall 2024 Issue)

(The) Ravens Perch
"Ghosted" (online March 10, 2024)
"Donation Tuesdays" (online March 10, 2024)
"Secret Faith" (online March 10, 2024)
"Genetics" (online May 15, 2024)
"In the Dark" (online May 15, 2024)
"Does Wanting Count?" (online May 15, 2024)
"The Golden Young" (online Aug. 28, 2024)
"The Love and Loss of a Dog" (online Aug. 28, 2024)
"The Way of Water Pots" (online Aug. 28, 2024)

Remington Review (Jan/Winter 2024)
"These Brave Branches"

Right Hand Pointing (*Ambidextrous Bloodhound Press*—Moral Injury Issue Dec. 24, 2023)
"All is Fair"

Rusty Truck Press (online May 12, 2024)
"An Adage of Untruth"
"Crawdads and Bologna"
"Counting Geese"
"Dear John Donne" (online Oct. 27, 2024)

(The) Rye Whiskey Review
"Kansas 1935" (online April 27, 2024)
"Bartender" (online July 20, 2024)
"My Father, the Lonely Mechanic" (online Aug. 12, 2024)

Scarred Tree (Moral Injury) Ambidextrous Bloodhound Press (online July 11, 2024)
"The Ballad of Returning Soldiers"

ACKNOWLEDGMENTS

Shot Glass Journal (Issue 42 Jan. 2024)
"The Grudge"
"Beginnings Triolet"

Snakeskin (online March 3, 2024)
"Our Cup of Coffee

Sparks of Calliope (online July 15, 2024)
"You Once Told Me I Was Beautiful"

Spill Words
"The Greatest Grief" (online Feb. 16, 2024)
"Upon This I Hitched My Dreams" (online Aug. 22, 2024)

Teach. Write (Fall 2024 Issue)
"Polishing Stars"
"The Kindness Experiment"

Third Wednesday Magazine (online July 7, 2024)
"The Blind Man's Nose"

Tipton Poetry Journal
"Line in the Sand" (Issue 59 Winter 2024) *featured poem of issue
*nominated Best of Net
"My Conversation with an Earthworm" (Issue 60 Spring 2024)
"Did I" (Issue 61 Summer 2024)

Toasted Cheese Lit Journal (Dec. 2023 Issue 23.4)
"Forever Eighteen"
"I Used to"

Well Read Magazine (online April issue 2024)
"Leftovers"

Westward Quarterly (Summer 2024)
"Running Late"

Acknowledgments

Wilderness House Literary Review (online Oct. 1, 2024)
"After Apocalypse"
"Delivery People"
"There's Something about the Rearview"

Visions International (Spring/Summer 2024)
"Lost Libraries"

About the Author

Arvilla Fee has been married for over twenty-two years to Colonel James Fee and has six biological, officially (and unofficially) adopted children and three grandchildren—all of whom she counts as her greatest blessings. She has had a long academic career, receiving a bachelors degree in the science of education from IUPUI, a masters of education from Weber State, and a masters of liberal arts English from Auburn University at Montgomery. She has taught English for over twenty-two years and has been published nationally and internationally in numerous presses including *Contemporary Haibun Online, Drifting Sands Haibun, Remington Review, Shot Glass Journal, North of Oxford, Mudlark, Havik, Gyroscope, Rat's Ass Review, Modern Literature, Right Hand Pointing, Halcyon Days, Tipton Poetry Review, Teach. Write., Last Leaves Magazine, October Hill Magazine, Snakeskin, Sparks of Calliope, Rusty Truck Press, Rye Whiskey Review, The Ravens Perch, Poets' Espresso Review, Poetry Breakfast, Paddler's Press, One Art Poetry, Of Rust and Glass, Northwest Indiana Literary Journal, Literary Yard, Lothlorien Poetry Journal, Last Stanza Poetry, MacQueen Quinterly, The Hooghly Review, Homer's Odyssey Magazine, Green Silk Journal, GAS: Poetry, Art & Music, Five Fleas Itchy Poetry, Cholla Needles, The Coalition, Boats Against the Current, Anacapa Review* and others. Arvilla's stories and poems are often based on her own experiences and trauma as well as the experiences she has witnessed in others. Some poems are fictional, coming straight from her imagination, although even a few of those contain tiny pieces of truth. Writing helps Arvilla make sense of

About the Author

her world and the larger world around her, and the *humanness* of her poems is designed to make readers feel part of the whole.

www.ingramcontent.com/pod-product-compliance
Lightning Source LLC
Chambersburg PA
CBHW050143170426
43197CB00011B/1938